Great Texas Birds

John P. O'Neill

GREAT TEXAS BIRDS

EDITED BY SUZANNE WINCKLER

UNIVERSITY OF TEXAS PRESS  AUSTIN

REQUESTS FOR PERMISSION TO REPRODUCE

MATERIAL FROM THIS WORK SHOULD BE SENT TO

PERMISSIONS, UNIVERSITY OF TEXAS PRESS,

BOX 7819, AUSTIN, TX 78713-7819.

∞ THE PAPER USED IN THIS BOOK MEETS THE MINIMUM

REQUIREMENTS OF ANSI / NISO Z39.48-1992 (R1997)

(PERMANENCE OF PAPER FOR PRINTED LIBRARY MATERIALS).

LIBRARY OF CONGRESS CATALOGING-IN-PUBLICATION DATA

O'NEILL, JOHN PATTON, 1942 –

      GREAT TEXAS BIRDS / ILLUSTRATIONS BY JOHN P. O'NEILL ;

   EDITED BY SUZANNE WINCKLER. — I ST ED.

            P.   CM.

      ISBN 0-292-76053-1 (ALK. PAPER)

      1. BIRDS — TEXAS.   2. BIRDS — TEXAS — PICTORIAL WORKS.

   I. WINCKLER, SUZANNE, 1946 –   .   II. TITLE.

   QL684.T4054   1999

   598'.09764 — DC21   98-47137

Title page painting: Long-billed Thrasher (unfinished).

DESIGN AND TYPOGRAPHY BY GEORGE LENOX

*For my parents, Kate and Haylett O'Neill, who endured dead birds
in the freezer, live ducks in the bathtub, and even a recently expired
spotted skunk in the kitchen, and still encouraged me,
and for Don Eckelberry and George Sutton, who showed me
that light and life can be portrayed on paper.* JPO

Contents

Preface

I HAVE THE GOOD FORTUNE to have in my possession one of the paintings in this book. In the early days of this project, Edgar B. Kincaid Jr. purchased *Scissortail Flycatcher and Texas Bluebonnets* from John and gave it to me. My interest in birds stems in large measure from the influence of Edgar, who was a lifelong bird watcher, editor of the book *The Bird Life of Texas,* and, I believe most people would agree, the éminence grise of Texas birding until his death in 1985.

The *Scissortail Flycatcher* now stands in my stairwell, where every day I can attach to it my own private narratives. It tethers me to Edgar and to Texas. More than a decade ago, John O'Neill asked me if I would write a text to accompany an assemblage of paintings he was working on, the subject being his favorite Texas birds. I agreed, and, to borrow an appropriate image from the poet Charles Bukowski, the days ran away "like wild horses over the hills." A certain fright came over me when I realized I might have to write this text. I could not pose as an authority on Texas birds. I could no longer claim to be a Texas birder. I've hardly birded in Texas since I left in 1985. And I did not want to appropriate these images by telling people what they mean to me. (On page 94, I have said a few personal things about the Yellow-breasted Chat.)

It seemed to me, however, that this body of work was about more than birds. As John painted, it was as if he were building a house in which there were many people. It contained friends and colleagues—mutual, his, and mine. It was a house full of people for whom birds, especially Texas birds, loom large. These people study bird behavior, taxonomy, physiology, evolution, ecology. They take people around the world to see birds. Bless their hearts, they work to conserve avian habitat and teach people young and old not just about birds but about the biologically rich world we live in. They simply love to be outdoors looking at birds.

These were the people who could rightfully speak about these paintings, and so we asked if they would. Roger Tory Peterson was among those who agreed, but failing health and his death in 1996 prevented his contribution. It is probably the first and only time he failed to fulfill an assignment pertaining to birds.

Here are fifty people, all writing about a bird with special meaning to them. We even commandeered, without their permission, two dead people—Roy Bedichek and Edgar Kincaid. Some of us are windy, some shy, some straight to the point, but we are all friends and we all care about birds. And John has painted a lovely edifice where we can be together.

SUZANNE WINCKLER
Omaha, Nebraska

PUBLICATION OF THIS BOOK WAS MADE POSSIBLE THROUGH
THE GENEROSITY OF THE FOLLOWING SPECIAL PATRONS
AND CONTRIBUTORS.

NELDA C. AND H. J. LUTCHER STARK FOUNDATION
THE MUDGE FOUNDATION, IN HONOR OF THE LATE EDMUND W. MUDGE III
DR. AND MRS. DON CONNELL
MR. AND MRS. B. D. ORGAIN
H. IRVING SCHWEPPE, JR., M.D.
RAE V. ANDERSON
MARVEL W. ORGAIN

Acknowledgments

DURING THE TEN YEARS in which I painted the portraits published here I basically lived by selling the original works as each was finished. As any artist knows, a steady flow of paintings for clients who pay their bills on time is the way he or she keeps going. In most cases the person choosing a particular species from our list did not know what the final piece would look like until it was delivered—I let the client pick the species, but I was usually responsible for picking the plant or other background material. In some cases the recipient asked for the inclusion of a particular plant or object, based on a personal experience with the bird, and sometimes I chose something to go with the bird that I knew had a personal touch to it. This is part of what made the project enjoyable, and I am most grateful to all who bought my work and gave me the freedom to compose their painting or paintings.

In traveling across Texas I was given access to private land where I could study birds, without having to constantly stop and tell people what I was doing, away from the hustle and bustle of highways. I am most grateful to Pete and Irving Schweppe for access to land in Atascosa County, to Marvel W. Orgain for access to her ranch in Kerr County, and to A. R. Guerra and family for access to the Guerra Brothers ranches in Hidalgo County. All of these areas are among my favorite parts of the state. I also enjoyed being able to visit both state and federal lands, especially Big Bend National Park in the Trans-Pecos, Santa Ana and Laguna Atascosa National Wildlife Refuges, and Bentsen–Rio Grande Valley State Park in the Valley, as well as many other places, among them numerous roadsides, across the state.

Although it is fun to paint outdoors, it is rarely practical. The need for reference material was critical, and I thank James V. Remsen, curator of birds, and Steven W. Cardiff, collections manager, of the Louisiana State University Museum of Natural Science for access to the specimens in the outstanding collections housed there. They kindly responded to my requests—requests that often had "ASAP" attached!

Since the paintings were to be delivered to their owners as they were completed, I had to rely on having 4″x 5″ transparencies made of each as it was done. For this I am most grateful to Jim Zeitz of the LSU Public Relations Office; in the early days he was willing to experiment with film and lighting in order to get the colors critically balanced, resulting in a "reproduction-quality" transparency. His colleague Prather Warren helped with other necessary photography, and I thank both of them for their assistance.

Eleven of the paintings were done for the Louisiana State University Museum of Natural Science and are owned by that institution. One was purchased by the Hill Memorial Library at LSU. I am most appreciative that they are available for inclusion in the book.

The remainder of the paintings were commissioned or purchased by individuals during the book project, and I am most grateful to the following, without whose interest and support there would have been no book:

Leticia A. Alamía, Rae V. Anderson, Mr. and Mrs. Richard Barrows, Stephen Chang, Dr. and Mrs. Don Connell, Mr. and Mrs. William M. Ferguson,

Kenneth W. Fink, Mr. and Mrs. Charles W. Frank, Mr. and Mrs. Charles Fryling, Nita Fuller, Gulf States Utilities, Mr. and Mrs. David T. Hamilton, Edgar B. Kincaid Jr., Mr. and Mrs. Hilaire D. Lanaux, Greg and Cheryl Lasley, George Lenox, Bruce Maxwell, Terry Maxwell, Reed S. Morian, Sally Morian, Mr. and Mrs. B. D. Orgain, Marvel W. Orgain, Dr. and Mrs. Thomas E. Pope, Mr. and Mrs. John T. Schulenberg, Dr. and Mrs. H. Irving Schweppe, Mr. and Mrs. John Trott, Lucy Waskell, and Janice A. Wyrick.

I am also most grateful to the people who agreed to write the species accounts. I want to personally thank each one for his or her contribution.

Lastly, but certainly not "leastly," I want to give special thanks to the staff at the University of Texas Press. Shannon Davies, our editor, liked our idea and stuck with us in the slowest of times. We are glad that she will now be able to hold a copy of the book in her hand!

JOHN P. O'NEILL
Baton Rouge, Louisiana

Introduction

W HEN YOU ARE BORN IN TEXAS, you grow up knowing you are different. After all, the state is the largest in the lower forty-eight, and everyone firmly believes that *everything* is bigger and better here than in any other state. It may be stretching the truth to say that all things are truly bigger and better, but when it comes to ecological diversity the facts speak for themselves. Where else can one travel from lush eastern deciduous forests to aspen and spruce woodlands near the peaks of mountains more than eight thousand feet high, or from seemingly endless short-grass prairies to tropical woodlands of trees with exotic names like *brasil, anacua,* ebony, and *guayacán*? And for relief from summertime heat there is always a trip to beaches along the 624-mile Texas Gulf Coast, much of which is composed of marshlands protected by some of the longest barrier islands in the world! A state with such an incredible diversity of habitats has a corresponding diversity of organisms, and none are more obvious than are its birds. More than six hundred species have been recorded within its borders—more than in any other state in the Union, including Alaska.

As a child growing up on the western side of Houston, I was fortunate to be able to get out in the woods and fields near my home and discover the wonder of the birds of that region. The Texas Gulf Coast not only has a diverse resident avifauna but also lies within an area traversed twice annually by one of the largest concentrations of migratory birds in the world. I will never forget the experience of coming home from school after a spring thunderstorm and finding half a dozen full-plumaged adult male Rose-breasted Grosbeaks in my backyard, or that autumn day when the first strong cold front came through and five hundred Broad-winged Hawks chose to spend the night in the trees by my home. After learning about the local birds, I began seeking new and exotic places to look for others. At first it was the nearby coast, but soon I was lured by the tropical woodlands of the lower Rio Grande Valley with their Green Jays, Red-billed Pigeons, Altamira Orioles, and other exotic species, and then by the excitement of the Big Bend area, where Colima Warblers (which nest nowhere else in the United States) and Band-tailed Pigeons, Phainopeplas, and Gray-breasted Jays were calling me to visit. I was fortunate to be able to go birding with many friends through the years, to experience most of the habitats in Texas, and to see most of the state's birds.

I began painting birds when I was about five, copying a picture of a bantam chicken to give to my mother. My dedication to painting birds has never waned—I even chose the University of Oklahoma as my undergraduate university because of the presence of George Miksch Sutton, one of the world's most talented painters of birds. Today, painting remains an integral part of my profession.

Although my research interests are primarily concerned with the distribution, ecology, and systematics of neotropical birds, and I have studied mainly those of Peru for the past thirty-five years, I still take great delight in looking at and studying Texas birds. The rush to find new species for my "life list" has slowed, but the sheer beauty of birds like the Black-throated Sparrow, the Green Jay, or the Northern Cardinal cannot be outdone by any bird anywhere in the world.

I can't remember when I first met Suzanne Winckler, but we have both had many similar experiences with birds in Texas and have carried our love of these creatures well into our adult lives. We both had a desire to do something in the way of a book that would express our feelings about a selection of incredible Texas birds that seemed to stand out among all the species found in the state. In 1986 we learned of each other's interests and decided to do a book that we would tentatively call "Great Texas Birds." I was a painter and Suzanne a writer—we could each do our part and get the project completed in about three years. We decided that each of us would begin by listing our favorite or "greatest" species and then compare the lists. We were only slightly surprised to find that our lists were about 75 percent alike! Certainly there is a core of Texas birds that most people would consider, for one reason or another, to be GREAT!

Neither Suzanne nor I thought that we would encounter as many interruptions in our personal schedules as we did, but that is how life is; our three-year estimate turned into a ten-year reality. As is usual with this sort of project, I am sure we both agree that the final product is actually much better for the amount of time that has passed since its inception. Having a good reason to revisit a number of places in Texas was probably one of the best parts of doing this book. Suzanne came up with the novel idea of asking Texas birders and ornithologists to share their knowledge and experiences by writing one species account each. As a result, not only did I get to see many birds again while painting the pictures, but I also got to visit and revisit a lot of wonderful friends around the state. We hope you will enjoy the results of our efforts!

JOHN P. O'NEILL
Baton Rouge, Louisiana

Great Texas Birds

Brown Pelican *Pelecanus occidentalis*

WEDNESDAY, DECEMBER 28, 1977, is a day I will never forget. About nine o'clock that morning Royce Pendergast of Orange, Texas, and I saw a single Brown Pelican turning large circles high in the air over the East Bay arm of Galveston Bay.

Royce and I were participating in the Bolivar Peninsula Christmas Bird Count, and what we saw was nothing short of a miracle. This was the first Brown Pelican seen on the count during the fifteen years since its inception in 1962. That lone individual marked a tentative and welcome beginning to the bird's recovery on the upper Texas coast, where it had historically been abundant.

By now, most people are aware of the Brown Pelican's nearly total extirpation from the Gulf Coast, brought about by environmental contamination with DDT and other chlorinated hydrocarbon pesticides. The chemicals caused direct mortality among adult birds and essentially eliminated reproduction because of eggshell thinning. This alarming consequence was first noted in the early 1950s, and by 1958 the species was just about gone from Texas.

Equally well known is the Brown Pelican's recovery following a ban on the use of the chemicals in the United States. Initially, the recovery was very slow—ten years passed before Brown Pelicans were next seen on the Bolivar Peninsula. Now they are seen on every trip to the coast and have been reported on each Christmas count since 1987.

The return of the Brown Pelican to the Gulf Coast is one of the real success stories of American conservation. Although their numbers are not yet back to pre-DDT levels, they seem to be moving in that direction. It is not unusual to see a hundred or more at one time resting on the Bolivar Flats. But for me, none of the present-day flocks has the significance or provides the thrill of that lone bird of 1977, flying high over East Bay, indicating that, just maybe, things were going to get better.

BILL GRABER

Green Heron and Black Willow *Butorides virescens* and *Salix nigra*

T HE ADULT GREEN HERON is a small, dark heron with yellowish legs. It has a glossy, blackish-green crown, which can be raised to a shaggy crest. The sides of the neck are a conspicuous rich chestnut color, with the back and wings having a slaty green or blue-green appearance. The Green Heron is a small bird; at a length of about eighteen inches, it is only slightly larger than the Least Bittern. Its overall shape is chunkier than the bitterns and other herons.

The most common vocalization of the Green Heron is an *akee-ow* or *akee-onk,* usually uttered when it becomes alarmed.

As a rule, the Green Heron does not nest colonially like other herons. Instead, this species prefers the solitary haunts of dense shrubbery or low trees, usually out of sight of predators and other birds. In Texas, the Green Heron is a common migrant and summer resident—except in the Trans-Pecos region, where it becomes an uncommon and local breeding bird. In most Texas winters, it retreats to coastal habitat and is generally found inland only in South Texas.

The Green Heron does not usually move through the shallow water to feed, as do many other herons. It is most frequently observed perched motionless above still water on a low branch or shrub. There it waits in Zen-like fashion for a small fish or invertebrate to pass under it. At just the right moment it will slowly extend its neck and, with a lightning-quick thrust, stab at its prey.

JIM PETERSON

Reddish Egrets *Egretta rufescens*

THE REDDISH EGRET is more tied to coastal bays and beaches than is any other New World heron. Rarely straying inland, even during postbreeding dispersal, this great Texas bird makes its modern stronghold on the Texas coast, where it comes in two colors: the dark (reddish) morph and an infrequent white.

Based on his observations of habitat destruction in Texas and Mexico, Edgar B. Kincaid, mentor to a covey of young Texas birders in the sixties and seventies, counseled us to anticipate the continual decline of many bird species. After a brush with extinction, *Egretta rufescens* has managed to dodge Kincaid's forecast and even make a slow recovery of late.

First there was the commercial millinery trade, which peaked at the beginning of the twentieth century. Heavily affected throughout its Gulf and Caribbean range, the Reddish Egret was completely extirpated from Florida by plume hunters, who shipped as many as 130,000 egret and heron skins in a single load to New York and Europe for use in fashioning women's hats! Not only did it take 150 to 1,000 skins to obtain a kilogram of the coveted "aigrettes" (the silky display plumes that gave the group its name), but the birds were also harvested at their breeding colonies, further multiplying the damage. And we're talking tens of thousands of kilograms— millions of egret skins. What percentage of those were Reddish Egrets is anyone's guess (worldwide, Great, Snowy, and Little Egrets were most affected), but recolonization of Florida by Reddish Egrets has been incremental, reaching 275 pairs by the early nineties.

In Texas, well after recovery from the plume-hunting days—and thanks largely to National Audubon Society warden protection of some of the major coastal heronries—further unexplained declines occurred through the sixties, from estimates of 3,200 pairs in 1939 to 550 pairs by the mid-sixties. By the mid-seventies, when I worked as General Land Office biologist with the Texas Fish-Eating Bird Survey, the Reddish Egret population had climbed back up to an estimated 1,400 to 1,600 pairs, a level that it has maintained, with fluctuations, to the present—much to the delight of Texans and (now) birders worldwide.

To watch the Reddish Egret prancing and dancing and strutting on the flats around its Gulf and Caribbean homeland, one would think it had on earphones playing pure Bob Marley. This aberrant foraging behavior, unique among the herons—indeed, among birds—was the taxonomic rationale for placing the Reddish Egret in its own monotypic genus, *Dichromanassa*. It has since joined the company of other egrets in the genus *Egretta*. Ornithologists have offered descriptions of this feeding behavior, such as "wing-flicking," "foot-raking," and "canopy feeding," but these terms fail to convey the wild abandon of a Reddish Egret feeding on the flats.

If you are what you eat, then a Reddish Egret is a sheepshead minnow, a white mullet, a pinfish, a long-nosed killifish—perhaps even a frog, a tadpole, a crustacean, or a dragonfly. But a Reddish Egret is not what it eats; it is much, much more. It's the partial embodiment of all that is right with the world: a sea breeze, open tidal flats, distant horizons. This is a bird for whom life truly is a beach.

ROSE ANN ROWLETT

Roseate Spoonbills *Ajaia ajaja*

MAY YOU HAVE THE GOOD FORTUNE to encounter Roseate Spoonbills on the drabbest possible day, when the bays and back-island marshes of the Texas coast have been leeched of their color by a furious white sun, or by gray banks of wintry cloud. The water, which can sometimes be brilliant, will on this day be as lusterless as the mudflats. Late in the afternoon, near dusk, you will happen to lift your eyes and there they will be, gliding single file in perfect silence above the saltgrass, bringing a shocking blast of color to that monochromatic gloom.

When they are not in flight, when they are merely stalking about in the water or roosting in the tangled vegetation of some scrubby spoil island, Roseate Spoonbills may not strike a casual observer as particularly beautiful birds. Though their wings and shoulders are washed with pink, their plumage is mostly white—sometimes a dirty white—and their greenish heads are as bare as the pates of vultures. Their bills flange out into a strange flattened oval at the base. This "spoonbill" is no blunt instrument but an extremely sensitive probe, allowing the birds to sense shrimp and small fish as they sweep their heads back and forth in the murky water. A Roseate Spoonbill's vocalizations are few—a bit of grunting and cheeping now and then, and a seldom-heard baritone distress call that one authority describes as "undeniably weird."

In keeping with their alien appearance, the birds are given to indecipherable behaviors. On occasion, a group of spoonbills will spontaneously be seized by an impulse to extend their necks and peer up into the sky in blank contemplation, and then just as mysteriously the moment will pass and they will resume probing the water with their spatulate bills. The erotic and domestic lives of Roseate Spoonbills are so touchingly intertwined that both sexes appear to have a fetishistic attachment to nest-building materials. Nothing excites a male spoonbill more than a female rustling a twig with her bill, and all during courtship there is a great deal of handing back and forth of sticks. Sometimes, as a prelude to copulation, a male and female will grasp the same stick in their bills and fervently shake it until their excitement reaches such a pitch that they can stand it no more.

Because Roseate Spoonbills are so disposed to silence they do not announce themselves when they fly overhead, though if they are close enough you can sometimes hear the steady whup of their wings. They just always seem to appear out of nowhere at the moment when you are most receptive, when the light is at its most concentrated and precise. They fly with their necks outstretched, propelled by decisive wing strokes that sometimes climax in a gorgeous glide. At such moments their widespread wings are illuminated like a stained-glass window, the sun filtering through the lush primary and secondary feathers. An adult spoonbill in its full nuptial plumage, when seen from below, is almost completely suffused with color, with intoxicating permutations of pink and rose and carmine. Roger Tory Peterson is content to describe the overall hue as "shell pink." Other ornithologists are obsessive about deconstructing the spoonbill's elusive color, breaking it down into "hermosa pink," "la france pink," and "eosine pink." But it is an impossible thing to describe precisely, perhaps because the appearance of Roseate Spoonbills against the leaden coastal sky always feels glowingly unreal in the first place, as sumptuous and fleeting as a dream.

STEPHEN HARRIGAN

Black-bellied Whistling Ducks and Cattails

Dendrocygna autumnalis and *Typha latifolia*

IT WAS THE SUMMER OF 1961, and young Chip had just listened to a talk by Texas Parks and Wildlife Department game warden Frank Henze. As part of the requirements for Chip's studies for the nature merit badge, the session centered on a funny-looking duck named the black-bellied tree duck. Chip was a Tenderfoot Scout and was spending his first-ever week away from home at Camp Karankawa on the shores of what was then Mathis Lake, now Lake Corpus Christi. As he walked the meandering trail from the campsite to the dining hall later that day, he heard the ringing *pee-chee-chee-nee* of birds flying nearby. Suddenly a pair of the rare and beautiful black-bellied tree ducks came into view over the brush-lined trail. Chip, a budding bird watcher even at this tender age, was amazed. Here were the very birds he had seen in the cage at Mr. Henze's talk! Here were these rare Mexican ducks that were starting to spread northward into Texas.

Now recognized as the Black-bellied Whistling Duck, *Dendrocygna autumnalis* is also known in various locales of Texas and Mexico as Mexican squealer, *pato maizal, pichichi,* and *pijije.* The bird is an attractive one, characterized by a rich chestnut-colored breast that grades abruptly into the black belly that gives the species its common English name. Disproportionately long wings and neck further dignify this bird—or do they add an air of gangliness? The black wings are marked with white wing patches, and the legs and bill add a touch of color. The long, bare legs, pinkish orange, dangle down in front of the duck as it lands after flight. The bright, clownlike bill is pinkish red with orange between the nares, and blue at the tip.

This duck was formerly called a tree duck because of its propensity to perch and nest in trees, unlike many of our other ducks. In South Texas whistling ducks are often seen atop fence posts, on yucca blossoms, and even swinging precariously on the power lines that stretch along roadways. The name *pato maizal* confirms the food preferences of this fine duck. Literally "cornfield duck," the black-belly is very fond of cereal grains grown under agricultural conditions. In the spring and fall, large flocks are found in feedlots, "ankle deep" in flooded rice fields, in harvested milo and cornfields, and atop the grain elevators of the flat coastal plain.

This species is one of the wildlife success stories of the Southwest. Along with species like the White-tailed Kite, *Elanus leucurus,* the black-belly has spread northward from the Mexican border. In large part, the advance of the black-belly has been a direct result of the containment of water, from stock ponds to large flood-control reservoirs, coupled with the installation of nesting boxes for this species in proximity to these impoundments. Like its distant cousin the Wood Duck, *Aix sponsa,* the black-belly nests in natural cavities but will accept artificial housing when it is provided.

One interesting aspect of this species' colonization activities involves dump nesting. It is not at all unusual for a population of black-bellies to be so large that multiple females will lay their eggs in a single preferred cavity. Normally laying twelve to sixteen eggs each, the ducks will leave a multilayered pile of eggs for one hen to incubate. The eggs, the size of a small hen's egg, will not all receive sufficient heat for incubation in these dump nests. The bottom layers never develop at all, the middle layers may develop more slowly or not at all, and the top layers develop normally.

One such dump nest could be found in August of each year during the early 1970s on the west side of Lake Corpus Christi. The number of eggs in it would consistently reach seventy-five to eighty-five. This particular nest, however, had a problem. A very large bull snake, *Pituophis melanoleucas sayi,* would raid the cavity around Labor Day each year, leaving with twelve to fifteen of the top-layer eggs in its digestive tract. This incident illustrates the need to provide some kind of predator shield on artificial houses erected for this bird.

The Black-bellied Whistling Duck is a popular member of the North American avifauna, and it appears to have secured a permanent foothold within the state of Texas.

STEPHEN E. "CHIP" LABUDA JR.

Wood Ducks and Live Oak *Aix sponsa* and *Quercus virginiana*

SINCE THE WOOD DUCK nests in the hollow of a tree ten, thirty, or even fifty feet above the ground, the method of descent of the ducklings has been a matter of considerable controversy. Some say they climb up the hollow to the opening and simply tumble out. Others say the parents carry them to the ground. All except one observer agree that if the nest is above water, the ducklings tumble out.

Audubon *asserts* that the mother carries the ducklings down, but *records that he saw* them tumble from the nest. If they are carried, how does the parent carry them—in the bill or on the back? The back and the bill—each has its partisans and its eyewitnesses. Mr. [Arthur C.] Bent's correspondents have seen the wood duck in flight carrying the duckling, and they have seen the duckling carried in the bill and between the feet, as well as on the back. Dr. T. S. Roberts inclines to the tumbling theory and quotes Joseph Dixon's study in which out of twelve nests under observation, eighty per cent of which were over water, he actually saw the ducklings tumble out of three of the nests. None were carried. Those who have seen a little one riding on the back of the mother say that as soon as she gets over water she throws her body into a vertical position and thus dumps the duckling.

The anatomist makes his contribution by observing that the wood duckling is hatched with long, sharp toenails, which would seem to indicate that nature knew that he would immediately have some climbing to do. The duckling is also supplied with an unusual amount of down. He is described as an unusually fluffy duckling, which would seem to anticipate some sort of fall, but whether from the nest or from the mother's back or beak is not indicated. . . .

Of course, it is possible that two methods are used, but unlikely, since it is the nature of an instinct to discharge itself in a definitely restricted channel. There are few alternatives. Choice, the great stimulus of rational thinking, confuses instinct.

To me, the claws are the most marvelous thing about the whole story. Two days out of the shell, the duckling has developed claws long, sharp, and hard enough to enable it to climb a perpendicular wall of wood two to four feet high, roughly twelve to twenty-four times its own height. Coincidentally with climbing hooks it has developed enough feathers to break a fall of thirty feet. I am inclined to reject the carrying story, since folks like the motherliness of safe-conduct, especially by air, and resent the idea of a mother hard-hearted enough to call her babies off a high place to fall hit or miss, bumpity-bump, to the ground.

ROY BEDICHEK
Adventures with a Texas Naturalist

Swallow-tailed Kite and Bald Cypress *Elanoides forficatus* and *Taxodium distichum*

I F YOU LOVE BIRDS, as I do, you probably have a story similar to this one. Some birds have a mysterious way of getting all tangled up in the web of memories and motivations that become the framework of your life. By one small accident of time and place, the Swallow-tailed Kite got stuck in my life and drew me, through curious connections, into the thirty-plus years of bird watching and conservation that have now spun out to be my life.

During the spring and summer of 1975, when I was twenty-one years old, there were accidental sightings of Swallow-tailed Kites in the wet bottomland forests around Freeport, Texas. This was considered a very rare and exciting thing by my brother and other bird watchers of the area, a group of which I was outspokenly not one. But it promised to be a long and lonely summer in Houston, where I was home from college with a freshly broken heart, so I was more receptive than usual to joining the hunt for the exotic visitor and managed to overcome my too-cool-to-be-a-bird-watcher posture.

I quickly discovered that it was a major challenge to find a single bird, or even several birds, that have been glimpsed wandering over hundreds of square miles of swamp forest. Even one as big and bold as the Swallow-tailed Kite is elusive. I found myself immersed in reading about the haunts and habits of the rare visitor, looking for any clue that would help us pinpoint its whereabouts. From this, I learned the rudiments of ecology and came to appreciate the lyrical and quirky writings of nineteenth-century naturalists.

Armed with descriptions of potential nesting sites in enormous old trees and poetic visions of its graceful feeding sorties over the canopy of swampy forests, we sharpened our search. Mornings and weekends were filled with our quest to encounter this mysterious stranger. The search was energized by a sense of loss and a possibility of repossession. Although the kite had disappeared from most of its U.S. range, including Texas, perhaps now it was making a comeback.

The high point of the quest came in August, after months of unsuccessful searching, when my brother and I decided to jump the security fence and climb a three-hundred-foot water tower for a better look out over the canopy. This was not so many years after two high school friends had earned a trip to jail, and my eternal skepticism, for climbing a water tower to leave their mark of tribute to the homecoming queen. Now I found that my motivation had also elevated to a passion sufficient to risk life, limb, and pride. One hundred fifty feet above the ground, exhausted, hanging on to a narrow ladder with one hand and a twenty-pound camera lens with the other, I discovered a breathless addiction to adventure. It has not abated.

We never saw the Swallow-tailed Kite. The memories of that summer, of the time with my brother, of the friends we made and of the quest we shared, are perhaps stronger for not having found the bird. Certainly the thirst for exploring the natural world and an appetite for conserving it were ignited that summer. Both are now woven into my life in ways that I never planned. Ten years later, I realized that these things were so central to me that I could make a career out of them. The Swallow-tailed Kite became more than a bird; it helped define my entire life.

I saw the Swallow-tailed Kite two years later, long after I had given up the search in Texas. I was in a remote region of Mexico, on the border of Guatemala, with deep-blue lakes pockmarked in a volcanic landscape where the cones were shrouded in cloud forest and the valleys in pine trees. Montebello, it is called— the beautiful forest. Wheeling over the forest at the edge of a lake, a flock of five Swallow-tailed Kites were just as handsome and agile as I had imagined them in the heat of our summer quest. They were unexpected and the excitement was high and there was no prospect of ending the quest.

DAVID BRAUN

© John P. O'Neill - 1994

Harris's Hawk *Parabuteo unicinctus*

IN THE EYES OF MOST TRAVELERS, the South Texas brush country is forbidding and unforgiving. Everything has thorns, needles, or spikes. Yet, on a crisp December morning a number of years ago as my wife and I drove along an isolated Texas ranch road in Duval County, I remember how at home I felt in this ecosystem, often known as the Tamaulipan Thorn Forest. Far ahead of us on the crossbar of a telephone pole I saw two dark shapes side by side. I remarked to Cheryl that we were approaching two Harris's Hawks.

"How do you know they are Harris's Hawks?" she asked. "Well," I replied, "they are sitting right next to one another. Not many hawks do that." As we got closer, we stopped to watch the pair of hawks as the morning sun brought out the richness of their chocolate-brown breasts and bodies with bright rufous leggings and shoulders. As the hawks perched shoulder to shoulder, I remember Cheryl turning to me and saying, "I guess Harris's Hawks like to snuggle."

The Harris's Hawk is a medium-sized buteo that is one of the most characteristic birds of South Texas. In the United States, the species also occurs in parts of New Mexico and Arizona, but South Texas is really the bird's stronghold. It often forages on ground squirrels, wood rats, and other rodents in this thorn forest habitat, but it has also been known to take snakes and birds as big as night herons and ducks and is thought by some to feed on carrion from time to time. To folks from the eastern or northern United States, the word "forest" might seem a significant over-statement when they first view the ten-foot-high mesquite, acacia, and agarito scrub. A brief walk into these areas will, however, quickly demon-strate that the word "thorn" is very appropriate. This is the habitat that the Harris's Hawk loves.

Harris's Hawks have been described by some observers as having a dual personality, a sort of Jekyll-and-Hyde character. Usually the bird is seen sitting quietly, apparently watching the day go by with casual indifference. But when hunting, it transforms into an active and relentless predator. Some of its hunting habits seem more accipiter-like than buteo-like. I have watched these birds dive into the thorny brush with reckless abandon as they pursue a meal. Somehow the hawk pops out of the brush, none the worse from its thorny experience—and usually clutching its intended prey.

Harris's Hawks are residents of South Texas and can be found fairly commonly all twelve months of the year. There is evidence that some numbers of these birds withdraw into Mexico during the winter, but certainly a substantial percentage remains in Texas all year. They seem to be just as happy in 110-degree heat on a summer day as they are perched on a windmill in subfreezing temperatures when a blue norther marches through the state in the winter. Harris's Hawks hunt from a stationary perch or on the wing; they seem just as effective either way.

Each September there is an organized hawk watch near Corpus Christi, where observers tally migrant Broad-winged Hawks and other raptors as they move through Texas. It always surprises me when I pick up a dot with my binoculars, high in the sky, and I can see the characteristic white-black-white tail pattern of a Harris's Hawk. I've watched a Harris's Hawk soar with a migrant stream of Broad-winged or Swainson's Hawks as if enjoying the parade. As often as not, the Harris's will eventually drop away while I watch and return to more earthly altitudes and the thorn forest habitat it loves.

Harris's Hawks seem to enjoy each other's company far more than other raptors do. It is not unusual to find several birds hunting, resting, or just hanging around together. There are accounts of apparent cooperative hunting by several birds as they cruise over ponds and brush to flush prey. More often than not, if two or more hawks are perched on the same pole in South Texas, they will be Harris's Hawks.

As in most raptors, female Harris's Hawks are a little larger than males. When you see two Harris's Hawks sitting near one another you can often detect a noticeable size difference, probably indicating a mated pair.

Harris's Hawks appear to have increased their range somewhat in recent years. They are show-ing up with greater frequency in Central and even parts of North Texas. The species has even made appearances in Oklahoma and farther north. In November 1994, Cheryl and I were driving along a road in Cochran County, just west of Lubbock, an area far to the north of the typical Harris's Hawk range. But we found eleven of them within a one-mile stretch of road, and six were perched together in one small tree. I was amazed at this out-of-range discovery and kept pointing at the birds and saying to Cheryl, "Look, those are all Harris's Hawks!" She looked at me and calmly said, "Well, sure they are, and they are all snuggling together." And indeed they were.

GREG LASLEY

Crested Caracara and Yucca   *Caracara plancus* and *Yucca* sp.

THE DATE WAS SEPTEMBER 30, 1975, and I had just left Aransas after my first visit to that special national wildlife refuge during what would be a memorable first trip to Texas. I had been asked to come to Texas to make a series of appeals for several Catholic missions in the Houston area. The appeals were held on a number of consecutive weekends, so I had some free time on the intervening weekdays. For a Connecticut birder, only three years into the sport, this opportunity was akin to unleashing a young child in the proverbial candy store.

I had spent hours poring over Jim Lane's *A Birder's Guide to the Texas Coast* and planned to travel Route 774, as he suggested, toward Refugio on my way to the Rio Grande Valley. I had one thing on my mind at the time: Crested Caracara, my target species.

I half expected this strange member of the Falconidae to be somewhat difficult to find, so I was stunned to see one perched, high on a pole, exactly where Jim Lane said one should be. Or maybe I was stunned by the awkward beauty of the Mexican eagle, as it is sometimes called. All in all, I must have studied twenty-five or more caracaras before I reached Refugio.

Despite its phylogenetic proximity to the swift-flying falcons, the caracara—long-legged, long-necked, and heavy-billed—looks anything but falconlike. Indeed, its heavy but elegant flight is somewhat like that of the raven. Over time I learned that this crested raptor is as at ease on the ground as in the air. Fleet of foot, it commonly chases down prey, such as small mammals and reptiles. Rather opportunistic, it will also feed on carrion, scratch the ground for insects and bugs, dig through cow dung for beetles, and harass other birds until they drop or disgorge their food.

The bird's odd name is of Guarani Indian origin and is an onomatopoeic rendition of its infrequently uttered *cara-cara* cry. Although commonly seen in the coastal grasslands and brush country of South Texas, the caracara's greatest claim to fame is its place on the official seal and coinage of the Republic of Mexico, where it perches on a prickly pear, grasping a rattlesnake in its beak.

Five years after this birding trip to Texas I was offered an assignment in the Rio Grande Valley. I jumped at the chance to continue my ministry in a bird-friendly place. In the end I was always looking for two flocks.

FATHER TOM PINCELLI

Plain Chachalacas and Texas Sugarberry *Ortalis vetula* and *Celtis laevigata*

THIS PLAIN BIRD WITH the poetic name exists somewhere between the Scylla of a chicken and the Charybdis of a curassow. It's a good thing, too, because such asylum has protected most of the dozen or so species of chachalacas from the immoderate hunting pressure visited upon their larger, tastier relatives, the more ornate curassows and guans. Nor have they been subdued, as battery hens have. True, chachalacas are sometimes captured as nestlings and raised as pets, but they will not reproduce this one-shot domesticity. The docile Cracidae family is notoriously difficult to breed in captivity, and interspecific hybrids among the chachalacas themselves are virtually unknown. So the tale that these bantam guans are inter-bred with gamecocks to produce a superior strain beats cockfighting. No, these neotropical brush dwellers have suffered more from the cockamamie war on their habitat than from any open pit, oven spit, or cockpit.

This is especially apparent in the lower Rio Grande Valley, where the Plain Chachalaca has the distinction of being the only member of its family to make it north of the border—and just barely at that. Here the Cock-of-the-brush is doing its best in the corridor of willow and mesquite that hugs the Rio Grande in Starr County and in the few dense thickets of fragmented tall brush remaining—chiefly close to the river and its historic resacas; and then, predominantly in the parks and refuges—in Hidalgo and Cameron Counties, where it appears equally at home in the trees or on the ground. Normally wary, this Great Texas Bird becomes, in Bentsen–Rio Grande Valley State Park, cocksure, mounting a snowbird's feeder or untying the shoelaces of a Yankee. At the northern limit of its distribution, the Lone Star Chachalaca's safest haven is, I'm afraid, deep in the hearts of Texans, who are no doubt cheered by the news that it is faring better—for the time being—in other parts of its range.

Chachalacas are nonmigratory and are distributed throughout Middle America and across much of tropical South America in suitable habitat. The chachalaca that John has painted ranges south of the border along the Caribbean slope to Nicaragua (with an isolated population inhabiting the arid Pacific slope in northwestern Costa Rica). The other, margin-ally less plain members of this unornamented genus entertain those of us lucky enough to have made their acquaintance, but most folks have met only *Ortalis vetula,* one of the handful of birds boosted by every last chamber of commerce in the delta—or so it seems. Perhaps this is as it should be, since as a member of the glad-handing Cracidae, *O. vetula* is a most approachable ambassador and capable of an uproarious family welcome.

Unbearably loud if issued from nearby, the welcoming of morn (at a slightly more civilized hour than a rooster with something to prove) makes the Plain Chachalaca anything but plain, if by "plain" we mean ordinary. If we mean "obvious," I'll grant you it's plain and then some. Okay, the bird's uniform earth tones are responsible for its English given name. But its rowdy, rhythmic dueting and raucous group vocalizing are plainly responsible for the onomatopoeic surname. Males deliver the stentorian bass, females the strident soprano. One pair's initiating a powerful and repetitive *cha-ca-LAC!* from atop a mesquite serves as a challenge to another pair some distance away, whose resounding reply prompts yet another to up the ante: *slap-her-BACK! keep-it-UP! cut-it-OUT!* In short order, the thorn brush, still damp with the dew of morn, is reverberating with uncivilized reciprocity of a most ancient kind, well before the day heats up.

JOHN ROWLETT

©John P. O'Neill - 1995

Attwater's Greater Prairie-Chickens *Tympanuchus cupido attwateri*

EVER SINCE THE WHITE MAN FIRST encountered the Greater Prairie-Chicken, he has persisted in his efforts to exterminate it. During the twentieth century, direct slaughter has abated, but habitat destruction continues as Americans proceed to convert virtually every square mile of their country into highways, hamburger stands, and beer joints. . . .

First to go was the Eastern Greater Prairie-Chicken, usually termed the Heath Hen, *Tympanuchus cupido.* Extirpated on the north-eastern U.S. mainland in 1835, a protected (from hunting), inbred colony existed into the 1920s on Martha's Vineyard off the Massachusetts coast. . . . A living Heath Hen was last reported with certainty on March 11, 1932.

No attempt whatever was made to save the north central Texas population (which possibly numbered 500,000 birds circa 1850) of the Northern Greater Prairie-Chicken, *T. c. americanus.* Between 1870 and 1890, these birds were shot by the wagon load for meat and blood sport; even worse was the plowing up or overgrazing of their grassland habitat.

Along the Texas coast, the Attwater's Greater Prairie-Chicken, *T. c. attwateri,* was slaughtered with customary frontier abandon between 1870 and 1900. Competitive shoots with up to fifty contestants were regarded as great fun. Sometimes downed birds were eaten or sold; upon other occasions they were left to rot. For *attwateri,* as for other races, plowing under of the native sod was even more damaging than gunshots. Where overgrazing by livestock weakened the turf, huisache (*Acacia farnesiana*), mesquites (*Prosopis*), retama (*Parkinsonia oculeata*), and other brush encroached, reducing the acreage suitable for this prairie chicken. As of about 1880, the Attwater's was still generally distributed over the Texas coastal prairie from Colorado, Austin, Waller, and Harris Counties in the north to Orange and Jefferson Counties in the east (plus Cameron and Calcasieu Parishes in Louisiana), thence southwest to Goliad, Bee, San Patricio, and Refugio Counties—some 810,000 birds, according to V. W. Lehmann. . . . By 1937, the occupied area had shrunk to disjunct colonies within the area outlined above; at this time Lehmann determined that there were only about 8,700 *attwateri* in Texas—and in the world, since the last Louisiana record was on February 26, 1919.

According to biologists of the Texas Parks and Wildlife Department, there were 1,440 Attwater's Greater Prairie-Chickens in 1970, 2,212 birds in 1971, and 1,650 in 1972. In these three later years the only healthy concentrations were located in Austin, Colorado, Goliad, Refugio (the very best county, according to state wildlife biologists . . .), Victoria, and Wharton Counties, but there were a few remnant birds in Brazoria, Calhoun, De Witt, Galveston, Harris, Fort Bend, and Waller Counties. Two new (as of 1972) Attwater sanctuaries should slow the rate of decline. One is the World Wildlife Fund's 3,150-acre tract near Eagle Lake in Colorado County; the other is a 7,000-acre (of which 3,000 is good-to-fair prairie chicken habitat) extension of Aransas National Wildlife Refuge in Refugio County. It is becoming increasingly apparent that the Attwater's "Martha's Vineyard" will be Refugio County. The soil of Refugio is mostly very low-lying and salty. This condition has discouraged both the conversion of its grasslands into cotton, rice, and sorghum fields and the invasion of mesquite and other brush. *Attwateri,* in addition to being the southernmost grouse, is also the only one which lives under near–salt-marsh conditions. With careful protection and lots of luck, it is just barely possible that a few of these salty grouse may live to the dawning of the twenty-first century.

EDGAR B. KINCAID JR.
The Bird Life of Texas

EDITOR'S NOTE: In 1997, biologists estimated the wild population of Attwater's Greater Prairie-Chicken to be fewer than 100 individuals. Another 100 or so birds are part of a captive breeding program initiated in 1992 at Fossil Rim Wildlife Center. Since then, three other facilities have joined the program: Texas A&M University, the San Antonio Zoo, and the Houston Zoo. Release of captive-raised birds from these breeding facilities began in 1995. The goal is to rebuild the wild population to at least 5,000 individuals in several different areas by 2000.

©John P. O'Neill-1990

Northern Bobwhites *Colinus virginianus*

WHEN I FIRST READ Margaret Sanger's book *That Quail, Robert,* the Northern Bobwhite was one of the few birds I could identify (without a field guide) at my grandparents' summer house in New York. The story relates the adventures of an orphaned bobwhite quail who is lovingly raised by a New England family. The charming, pocket-size ball of brown-and-white fluff proceeds to enrapture everyone with whom she comes in contact. This true story has undoubtedly started many a child and adult on the road to wildlife appreciation, and so it may have been with me. By the time I moved to Texas, eighteen years ago, my birding skills had improved. Though another field guide was needed for the numerous new birds, one familiar voice welcomed me each morning to my new neighborhood. Actually, it wasn't necessary to hear his distinctive whistle to feel his presence. Quail Valley, Quail Glen, Quail Meadow, and innumerable other subdivisions, streets, and avenues in the area bore his name in one form or another. City councils eventually issued a ban on any new street names containing the word "quail"! Surely this was a promising statistic on bobwhite populations. Sadly, times change.

The last bobwhite quail I personally watched in my Houston neighborhood was in August 1983 during Hurricane Alicia. A single male, head pointed into the wind, struggled to maintain his balance on a raised berm in my yard. This unlucky fellow was undoubtedly blown in from elsewhere, as by 1983 urbanization was in full swing and it had been some time since I had heard any consistent bobwhite activity.

The bobwhite quail in Texas has been on a long-term decline over the past thirty to forty years. My one small observation of a disappearing population has been repeated time and again, especially in those urban areas east of the Piney Woods. Though the bobwhite was once hunted heavily for both food and sport, hunting did not have the devastating effect that habitat loss, agricultural chemical spraying, and the resultant scarcity of food may have exacted. Perhaps the bobwhite's ability to make a living on forest edges has allowed it to fare better than its cousins the prairie chicken, with whom it shares many similar requirements, though the bobwhite's status is by no means as imperiled as Texas' Lesser and Attwater's Prairie-Chickens.

The Northern Bobwhite has a wide range through North and Central America, its spread apparently limited only by northern cold winters and western arid climates. In Texas, there are two or three (depending upon whether you are a lumper or a splitter) races of bobwhite quail. They are commonly referred to as the interior bobwhite, *Colinus virginianus mexicanus* (southeast Texas); the plains bobwhite, *C. v. taylori* (north Texas); and Texas bobwhite, *C. v. texanus* (north central Texas). Differences in physical characteristics are subtle, and Texans, regardless of location, still hear the same plaintive whistle of bachelor males. A bobwhite by any other name is still a bobwhite!

Recently, I was amazed (on another reading of the Sanger book) at the vast number of different vocalizations heard and reported from "Robert" (in actuality a female); undoubtedly each sound had significant meaning (known only to other bobwhite quails but recognizable by Robert's human family). As a zoo professional, I know that both the natural and the admittedly unnatural behaviors observed by Robert's family were not "scientifically" recounted. I am reminded of a quote from Rachel Carson: "The lasting pleasures of contact with the natural world are not reserved for scientists but are available to anyone who will place himself under the influence of earth, sea, and sky and their amazing life."

The death of the last Heath Hen (a subspecies of Greater Prairie-Chicken) in 1932 was not a scientifically observable event. Its passing was noted by the absence of its distinctive call —an ominous warning for all of us who miss hearing the comforting harbinger of spring in many parts of Texas, the bobwhite quail.

ROCHELLE PLASSE

John P. O'Neill '95

Montezuma Quail, Mexican Pinyon Pine, and Copper Mallow

Cyrtonyx montezumae, Pinus cembroides, and *Sphaeralcea* sp.

IN TEXAS, MONTEZUMA QUAIL, also called Harlequin or Mearns Quail, live in open, evergreen woodlands of the southwestern Edwards Plateau, where they nest in late spring, and in similar habitat on mountain slopes in the Trans-Pecos, where a different population nests during the summer rainy season. Today's birds occupy only about one percent of their historical range in the state, now mostly private ranchland, and are protected from hunting. Their demise is linked to overgrazing. Montezuma Quail need grass a foot tall or taller as ground cover in a matrix of junipers, pinyons, and oaks at an elevation of about 1,500 to 6,500 feet.

This species differs from other quail in two ways that are important to its conservation. Individuals or small family groups prefer to crouch and hide in tallgrass rather than form large coveys and fly in the face of danger. And they specialize in digging up the bulbs of nut grasses (sedges) and wood sorrels with their strong feet and short, stout legs. The birds eat the fleshy parts of the bulbs, leaving the hulls in or near small holes. By comparing habitat that exhibits this telltale sign with similar habitat that does not, we can learn about the relative importance of grass cover to the quail's survival.

On the Edwards Plateau, my students and I studied nearby ungrazed and grazed ranches supporting Montezuma Quail and an over-grazed ranch no longer inhabited by the species. Tallgrass cover was the primary indicator of habitat at the grazed ranch, followed by fewer shrubs and greater soil depth. The ungrazed ranch was used only for hunting, so its tallgrass was more continuous, and deep, dry soil and hill slopes were indicative of bulb digging. The two inhabited ranches averaged 63 percent tallgrass ground cover, whereas the overgrazed ranch had only 25 percent tallgrass and relatively more short-grass and shrub cover.

Historical records suggest that Montezuma Quail thrived when herds of native grazers like bison, and even livestock, were unfenced. But overgrazing was not a widespread problem in those pioneer days, as it is today. Thus saving the birds on fenced ranchland is mostly a matter of keeping livestock at proper range capacity and rotating grazed and ungrazed pastures, leaving some habitat to the quail for several years at a time. Our studies in Central Texas and others in southeastern Arizona show that the ground cover of occupied habitat must be about 60 percent or more tallgrasses.

FREDERICK R. GEHLBACH

Wild Turkeys and Drummond's Phlox *Meleagris gallopavo* and *Phlox drummondii*

S DO ALL GALLINACEOUS BIRDS, Wild Turkeys prefer walking or running, never flying very high or far. Their habitat is wood-lands or brushy areas, into which, though they are large, they can disappear with extraordinary speed.

The Wild Turkey's historic range was from central Arizona to South Dakota, east to southern New England, then south to Florida, the Gulf Coast, and into Mexico. Turkeys have been introduced in California, Washington, Utah, Montana, Wyoming, South Dakota, Hawaii, New Zealand, and Europe. Apparently North American Indians used turkeys for food, but not to the extent that European settlers did. The domesticated version of this native species is now found worldwide.

In Texas the historic range was the eastern two-thirds of the state. Most were extirpated from the Panhandle and Piney Woods early in this century by hunting, habitat manipulation, and diseases from domestic poultry. Reintro-ductions by the Texas Parks and Wildlife Department have restored this largest game bird to those areas. Large landholdings in South Texas and the Edwards Plateau are apparently the stronghold of Wild Turkeys in the state. Since 1979, approximately 4,700 Eastern Turkeys, *Meleagris gallopavo silvestris,* have been introduced into eastern Texas, most after 1987. Rio Grande Turkeys, *M. g. intermedia,* have been restocked since 1933, with more than 32,000 released to 1995, 40 percent of those after 1980. Texas Parks and Wildlife is not planning any further restocking at this time.

Wild Turkeys live an average of two to three years, some as long as ten years. An average clutch is ten or eleven eggs; the incubation period is twenty-eight days. The nest is on the ground, with the hen doing all the incubating and caring for the offspring. The young can fly in about ten days and begin to roost in trees at about two weeks of age. According to a Texas Parks and Wildlife Department study, a turkey's diet, by annual percent volume, consists of 36 percent grasses, 29 percent insects, 19 percent browse, and 16 percent forbs.

Public areas where I have found Wild Turkeys easily include Aransas National Wildlife Refuge, Buffalo Lake National Wildlife Refuge, Choke Canyon State Park, Garner State Park, Lost Maples State Natural Area, Palo Duro Canyon State Park, Pedernales Falls State Park, and South Llano River State Park.

The one thing that stands out in my mind about Wild Turkeys, especially considering their large size, is how quickly they can disappear, particularly when I am trying to show them to someone.

EDWARD A. KUTAC

© John P. O'Neill - 1991

Sandhill Cranes *Grus canadensis*

IN THE CEDAR HILLS WHERE I LIVE, Sandhill Cranes are very much a part of our year, appearing dependably in autumn when cold fronts drive them south toward the Texas coast, and again in spring as they head back to northern nesting grounds. The long U-shaped skeins, often several within sight at once, pass over so high in clear skies that aging eyes like mine have to strain to pick them out, but they fly lower when clouds press them down toward the earth they seem to need to have in view. And always, from high or low, they sound the calls that bring you outdoors to squint upward, the grating, drawn-out croaks with which they communicate. Sometimes at evening, the croaks come faster as a flock circles and mills overhead, now flapping, now soaring—and debating, I like to think, the question of where the night's rest stop will be.

They are a reassurance, cranes, the survival of a large and visible natural force into a time when survivals of that kind have grown far less certain than they once were. I am no priest nor anything like one, but I find myself invoking a blessing on these great gray birds when they show up, every spring and every fall. May they endure.

JOHN GRAVES

John P. O'Neill - 1987

Purple Gallinule, Water Lettuce, and Cattails

Porphyrula martinica, Pistia stratiotes, and *Typha latifolia*

IN A WORLD LARGELY DEVOID of purple birds, the Purple Gallinule's visually arresting plumage demands notoriety. Surrounded by a host of secretive marsh dwellers clad in the browns and buffs of dry cattail stems, this glistening bird seems all the more remarkable.

Geographically aggressive, the Purple Gallinule has spread throughout the New World tropics. From there, numbers of them venture northward each year to nest in wetlands of the southeastern United States, including coastal Texas. Here, on ponds, reservoirs, or sluggish bayous mantled with floating vegetation, they are most likely to be seen after the first week of April. Breeding gallinules make good use of the region's long summer, and small chicks may be seen as late as September. By late October most have departed; only rarely does one linger into winter.

Invariably, this species is eagerly sought by visiting birders. In marshy East Texas, it is, unlike many other members of the rail family, readily observed. Using its unusually long, bright-yellow toes to distribute its weight, the gallinule openly navigates the floating leaves of water hyacinth, spatterdock, yellow lotus, and other aquatic plants, searching for seeds and small invertebrates. Its specialized toes are also well-suited for grasping branches, and they account for the species' decidedly arboreal habits. Rather than disappearing into tallgrass as so many of its relatives do, a Purple Gallinule may scurry up a clump of cane, or delicately ascend the branches of a willow or buttonbush. From there, it will survey an intruder, its tail pumping nervously. While it does so, its gleaming white undertail coverts seem to compete for attention with the red-and-yellow bill and powder-blue frontal shield.

With almost characteristic regularity, Purple Gallinules appear in strange locations and habitats, often well outside their usual range. For example, many land on ships at sea. This propensity to disperse, a genetic trait that they share with their Old World relatives, has produced colonies on far-flung islands. Locally, they are scarce beyond the coastal plain, finding little suitable habitat in arid West Texas. Migrants have been observed sharing the Gulf's shore with Sanderlings and Willets, and passing the night roosting high in the shade tree of a Houston yard.

ROBERT BEHRSTOCK

Ruddy Turnstone *Arenaria interpres*

SMARTLY GARBED AND CONFIDENT in demeanor, the Ruddy Turnstone possesses two special abilities: it procures food in an unusual way and it is able to migrate long distances. This nine-inch-long shorebird employs its wedge-shaped bill in tipping over beach pebbles and rooting in clumps of seaweed for invertebrates. Natural history illustrator of colonial America Mark Catesby (1682–1749) noted this activity in a turnstone he captured on his second visit to America, in May 1722. The bird came aboard Catesby's vessel bound for Charleston, South Carolina, about forty leagues off Florida's coast. The Englishman caged it, supplied stones, and noted how easily it used its strong upper mandible to flip them.

Fleet-footed, stocky, and ploverlike in shape, turnstones practice this food-gathering technique on beaches, shingle banks, and tide flats, though they may switch to eating berries on the Arctic tundras where they nest. Of the two species, the Black Turnstone is a Pacific Coast bird, whereas the Ruddy Turnstone is circumpolar in range.

Turnstones fly thousands of miles during seasonal migrations. Birds from Scandinavia and west Russia winter in Morocco and West Africa. Other populations from Arctic Canada and Greenland migrate eastward into the British Isles and the Iberian Peninsula. Still other birds from central Siberia winter along the Red Sea, the Indian Ocean, and southward to Cape Province, South Africa.

In the New World, Ruddy Turnstones winter all around coastal South America to Tierra del Fuego. A large concentration can be found in north central Brazil (from Belém to São Luís). There, researchers have tallied more than 17,900 birds (76 percent of the wintering South America population) on hard mudbanks along the indented shoreline. Smaller numbers congregate in Surinam and French Guiana.

Quitting these tropical and semitropical locations in spring, turnstones head along both the Atlantic and the Pacific Coasts toward northern nesting areas and begin to molt into cinnamon and black upperparts and gray underparts. Some fliers cross the Gulf of Mexico and head inland. They feed in marshlands along the Central Flyway, puttering, for example, on mudflats at municipal sewage facilities in Austin, Texas, or at Cheyenne Bottoms near Great Bend, Kansas.

I have seen them in Churchill, Canada, where on June 1 they flickered among ice floes in the Churchill River, piebald flashes against the snow. It is still bitterly cold then, but their guttural calls around the ponds near the town's grain elevator and fast flights along the river suggest an impatience to move on. They have another thousand miles to fly before establishing nest sites on coastal barrens, taking advantage of solitude and a short summer to raise their young. Thus, using the mid-latitudes as a way station and a corridor, turnstones link windswept tundras around ice-rimmed seas and mangrove-backed shorelines with their sure, swift, and direct passage.

ROBIN DOUGHTY

©John R.O'Neill·1985

Long-billed Curlew and Blue-eyed Grass

Numenius americanus and *Sisyrinchium angustifolium*

AN EERIE AND HAUNTING *CUR LEESE* rolls across the prairies of the Panhandle and echoes in the bays and marshes all the way south through the Laguna Madre. The sound is made by the largest shorebird in North America, with the longest and most bizarre beak. Cryptic brown, to live on the prairies and plains, but with flashes of burnt orange accented by dark primaries when it flies. And, oh, what a call. As wild and free as any sound of the wide-open spaces of Texas. And if Texas still encompassed the original area of the pre-1836 Mexican state, the bird would occur almost throughout, nesting in what is now Colorado, wintering in what is now the Mexican state of Tamaulipas. It is good to eat and was of considerable economic importance in the early years of Texas. This could have been our state bird.

I find the Long-billed Curlew to be one of the most interesting of all Texas' birds. A Great Plains prairie specialist, it nests on short- and midgrass prairies in the central United States and Canada and winters in South Texas and Mexico. Old traditional food-habit studies (postmortem examination of birds' crops) suggest that the bird relies heavily on grasshoppers and grass-hopper egg cases. Little information exists regarding winter food habits. In the upper Gulf Coast region of Texas, these birds frequent large open lawns near the coast. They are regular users of golf courses and ball fields. They are also found on bareground/salicornia areas above high-tide levels adjacent to bays. In extreme South Texas they utilize the Laguna Madre and are often seen wading in water up to their knees in the laguna. They also occur in the Katy prairie region west of Houston, where they seem to prefer fallow cornfields with the stalks plowed under.

What could they possibly be eating in these three distinctly different habitats? Is there something common to all three? What is their unusual bill good for in these diverse areas?

Recently, I watched a curlew in the fallow cornfield on the Katy prairie. It picked up several items with the deftness of a surgeon wielding forceps. Swallowed with an almost imperceptible motion, the items were obviously small ones that didn't require killing, tenderizing, or other preparation. Then the curlew lowered its posture and inserted its bill into a hole and with a jerk or two of its head produced what appeared to be an earthworm, in its upper bill near its mouth. It masticated the item a couple of times and swallowed. It picked a smaller item again, then inserted its bill in another hole—his time without results. It then probed beneath a cornstalk that was lying on the ground. Again it produced a large item that apparently was another earthworm. It strolled away from me at this point and I couldn't observe any other food items. I suppose the bill is best designed to probe worm holes, for either polychaetes or earthworms. I can't wait until I have an opportunity to observe curlews foraging in the other habitats. Next time I will count the items swallowed and the number of successful and unsuccessful probes.

FRED COLLINS

Black-necked Stilts *Himantopus mexicanus*

THE SHOREBIRDS OF TEXAS appear bleached and faded next to the prismatic warblers, tanagers, buntings, and orioles that overspread our coast in migrations. Our sandpipers blend with their decolored surroundings, often leaving footprints etched in soft sand as the only evidence of their passing. The exceptional Black-necked Stilt, however, demands attention.

The stilt is the antithesis of a shorebird, the extreme that defines the edges of what we conceive a shorebird to be. No muted colors here—it's brazenly black and white, precariously perched upon bubblegum-pink legs. No other shorebird in the state is more obvious or revealed.

The Black-necked Stilt is a locally common summer resident, nesting close to water in both coastal and inland wetlands. This species does not tolerate high salinity as well as some other members of its family, and coastal occurrences are normally limited to brackish rather than saline water. Along the coast it nests in marshes bordering sloughs and bays, in wet coastal prairie that has been burned by ranchers to provide new forage for cattle, and on the fringes of pools, ponds, and cattle tanks.

The stilt breeds inland on the playa lakes and around the countless reservoirs and ponds, fish hatcheries, rice fields, and sewage plants that mark the dispersion of humankind. These artificial wetlands have allowed the stilt to reach all corners of the state, with nesting noted as far west as El Paso and east to the edges of the Piney Woods. Range expansion aside, nowhere is the bird more common than along the coast and in the Panhandle. Inevitably, the stilt's range expansion in Texas will always be tempered by the absence or presence of those critical artificial habitats associated with people.

In late fall the stilt retreats to the coast, with the bulk of the Texas population migrating to the coastal marshes to our south. Over the past two decades the species has increased its numbers as a winter resident. Now many coastal marshes host small wintering flocks, but even the hardy stilts will leave the northern coast during an especially frigid spell.

Spring migrants arrive along the coast the first week of March, although the presence of wintering stilts makes the determination of exact early arrival dates impossible. Numbers increase rapidly through March and early April. By early summer coastal marshes and rice fields are replete with cackling, "broken-winged" parents protecting their young, which look like cotton swabs balanced upon matchsticks.

TED LEE EUBANKS

©John P. O'Neill · 1985

Least Tern *Sterna antillarum*

AS I WALK ACROSS A SHELL ISLAND used by boaters or fishers within the city limits of a coastal Texas community, the sky erupts with small, belligerent terns darting in front of my path through a once quiet colony. I keep walking to reach an unpopulated location where I can observe these, the smallest terns of North America. The Least Tern is pugnacious in defense of its nest site, where it takes on all comers—whether they be dogs, children, or interested gulls. Although I have never been struck by a defiant tern, I have on more than one occasion lowered my head in anticipation of a thump by a darting and diving adult.

The commotion of an unintended interruption finally subsides, and the adults slowly find their way back to their nest scrapes in the shell-and-sand substrate where one or two splotched and spotted buff-colored eggs reside. The scrapes, less than an inch deep, are surrounded with scattered objects discarded during courtship ceremonies. One adult (I cannot determine the sex) begins incubation once again. The colony returns to "normal."

Once the eggs hatch, the cryptically patterned young stay close by the scrape for only a day or two. Then they move off into nearby halophytic herbaceous vegetation, which the chicks seek for shade and protection. Just as often, young can be found "hunkered down" behind a piece of wood left from winter flooding. The chicks respond to alarm calls from adults in the colony by flattening themselves against the shell substrate and becoming for all practical purposes invisible. Nonincubating adult birds bring small topminnows from nearby foraging sites to feed newly hatched chicks.

Some may view these graceful, buoyant fliers found commonly along the Texas coast as sea swallows. To me the Least Tern is the "pugnacious pioneer" that any Texan would be proud of.

This bird has historically used the "newest," most inhospitable sites for colonies. These new habitats once occurred as emergent oyster bars in bays or along barrier beaches, or as sandbars created by a rampaging Panhandle stream. As long as the sites remained well above high tide or the rivers stayed in their courses, the terns continued to take advantage of the new land. These habitat pioneers will apparently return year after year to the same colony if the site remains free of extensive vegetation and free from severe disturbance by predators. In fact, some of the largest tern colonies along the coast have been found at sites where the birds have been protected from disturbance and vegetative growth has been retarded.

Unfortunately, traditional nesting habitats along the Texas coast are also coveted by humans for recreation and development. No longer is the graceful but pugnacious pioneer able to nest on Texas' barrier beaches and the shell bars of coastal bays. Instead it is mostly relegated to human-produced habitats. Now the scattered, loose colonies of Least Terns are more likely to be found on shell roads, gravel parking lots, or islands formed from dredged materials. The Least Tern has taken advantage of these human-produced habitats, but over time such areas may become ecological traps for this scrappy little bird.

DOUGLAS SLACK

White-winged Dove and Texas Ebony   *Zenaida asiatica* and *Pithecellobium flexicaule*

WHITE-WINGED DOVES were calling from trees all around our neighborhood when we moved to Austin in 1995. "Who cooks for *you?* Who cooks for *you?*" they asked and echoed again and again. The other birds I heard—cardinals, Carolina Wrens, titmice, and grackles—were familiar from my childhood in and near Fort Worth, but the dove's voice was new. It told me that even though I had returned to Texas, I was on new ground; this was a new start, this was Austin, of which I knew very little. I had never explored or birded here. I had never shared living quarters with so many large cockroaches or swatted so many tiny mosquitoes.

In time I learned that the White-winged Dove is also a recent arrival to Austin. Historically, Texas whitewings were limited to the Trans-Pecos region and the lower Rio Grande Valley, where they were at the northern edge of their breeding range. The Valley birds thrived in the tall brushlands of mesquite, ebony, huisache, and prickly pear that defined the region before clearing for citrus and other crops began earlier in this century. Before large-scale agriculture, there were records of fall flocks that included as many as a million birds. A portion of that whitewing population endures, for the birds have adapted to nesting in mature citrus and shade trees as well as in fragments of brushland. Their numbers dip considerably now whenever the citrus trees die back after freezes, but even at lower numbers they attract a crowd of hunters each fall for a shooting season that usually lasts only four half-days.

In recent decades, whitewings have expanded their Texas breeding range northward to urban centers like San Antonio, Austin, and now Waco, Brownwood, and even Amarillo. The birds in Central Texas cities have settled in as year-rounders, proliferating quickly where they find mature trees, water, well-stocked birdfeeders, and winter temperatures that are usually several degrees warmer than those of the surrounding countryside. So far, the White-winged Doves seem to have found their niche without displacing other birds. Mourning and Inca Doves still hold their own; in fact, from a doctor's office in Austin I have watched all three doves sharing birdseed on a wide concrete sill.

"Who cooks for *you?* Who cooks for *you?*" This year I know the whitewings: their silhouette on a power line, their feeding spots in our backyard, their silence in the late summer and fall, and their coos and croons that begin before light on spring mornings. "Who cooks for *you?*" they ask and ask. Some days the weary housewife in me mutters back under her breath, "*Nobody* cooks for me, *nobody!*" or the savage chef in me ponders how a few urban whitewings might be quietly transformed into dinner. But most days I delight in what is now a reassuring and familiar cadence, which works its way into my heartbeat so smoothly that I find it there even as I fall asleep at night.

SALLY GRAVES JACKSON

Greater Roadrunner and Texas Prickly Pear

Geococcyx californianus and *Opuntia engelmannii*

TRANSLUCENT LEAVES, tender chartreuse and filled with light, shimmered in a hot wind. Buzzing, immersed in brilliance, the desert waited for pollen to gather. Tiny claws skittered somewhere in luminous shadows, a White-winged Dove rattled in dry brush, but little else stirred at noon. The campground was empty except for myself, I thought, until an eerie clicking, deep and solid, split the silence. Then the voice appeared, throaty, familiar, each note descending in pitch, yet without visible form.

I had heard it often in that dry cactus land, wide-spaced with legions of pungent larrea, spiny lechuguilla and ocotillo, brittlebush, fragrant herbs, forgiving grasses, mesquite, and all their arid allies. But I had never seen the maker in the act. I hung motionless, wrapped in a Oaxacan hammock, suspended in transparent, hallucinogenic heat, reduced to the still consciousness of that radiant place.

He must have taken me for harmless, or else I really did disappear in that clear moment. Alert, dignified, with dapper tail at attention, he stepped smartly out of allthorn and flexed a handsome crest. His red-and-blue-bordered eyes scanned the world of our clearing, but I was only a flicker in his gaze. He advanced right up to a massive prickly pear and plucked a long, thin walkingstick from a fat pad. He deftly racked the legs against a spine and then ingested the body whole.

The long tail flicked again, the posture quickened, and he darted low, like flowing water, straight to a basking lizard. A short struggle, a snap of the head, and a precious gift hung limp from the powerful beak. I had read about this erotic event but had never seen it. The lizard is an essential ingredient of the alchemical potion that a male roadrunner is obliged to bring his intended bride.

The female must have the lizard or like sacrifice, I hear, to make sound eggs. All the shining energy gathered by the chosen one over a lifetime, all that it had eaten, all that crawled or flew or swam, or simply grew rooted in thin soil—all of that condensed into the act of procreation. We really are what we eat, and when finally eaten, become part of the feast at life's table. We are our habitat, physically, mentally, and, I daresay, spiritually. All at once alive.

As I lay in my hammock watching the ancient drama played out in the real time of dancing feathers and iridescent scales, the roadrunner and the lizard opened my eyes a little wider to the marvelous gift of being. He did not wait long with his trophy, but spun on wonderful feet with two toes forward and two back, perfect for speeding over flat or rugged terrain.

Although its lovely white arced wings serve well enough for it to rise suddenly above the scrub growth, then plunge like an arrow into concealment, the roadrunner is no aerial acrobat. No elite Epicurean either, this omnivore goes for diversity, nothing less than the whole cornucopia that is its home. The roadrunner is the Chihuahuan Desert, Sierra Nevada foothills, Arizona sagebrush, Texas scrub, Arkansas meadows, Louisiana thickets, Oklahoma prairies, Kansas grasslands, New Mexico plains, Old Mexico plateaus. Innocent, imparting pure awareness, it boldly holds that peculiar *paisano* point of view for the whole universe as it yearns to know itself.

JIM BONES

Elf Owl and Mesquite *Micrathene whitneyi* and *Prosopis glandulosa*

BIRDING IN THE VALLEY has always been exciting, primarily because of the tantalizing idea that almost anything is possible. In recent years more and more avid birders have come to scour the backroads and few remaining stands of brushland, hoping to get lucky and stumble across yet another great new bird for themselves and for South Texas.

In 1960, the birding possibilities were equally exciting. The few resident birders were hard-pressed to cover the area, however, and many parts of the Valley were checked only during official bird counts. Some species reported by early naturalist explorers had not been seen since the 1800s and were considered either extirpated or the result of incorrect collecting localities. This was believed to be the case with the Elf Owl.

After the annual spring bird count on May 1, 1960, the Luke McConnells of Mission, Texas, went home determined to find a Ferruginous Owl that night before the count period ended. They called later that evening to report that a different little owl was calling and flying in their backyard. We rushed to Mission and stood quietly in the darkness listening to the whimpering, puppylike calls and watching the tiny bird flit from the mesquite trees above us to the woodpecker hole in a pole beside a storage building. When the bird finally paused for a moment, we turned the beam of a powerful flashlight toward it and like a giant moth it gently fluttered down the beam of light and perched immediately above my head. The branch was gently pulled down, and I reached up and captured the first Elf Owl found in South Texas since March of 1894. What a thrill!

Later, exploring a road near the river at Roma, we found a brush area where old abandoned telephone poles lined the road. These poles had first served as nesting sites for Golden-fronted Woodpeckers; now the holes were being used by Elf Owls. A few mimicking whistles and the tiny owls would come bustling out to glare at the invaders. Many a bird watcher saw his or her first Elf Owl on this lonely road.

Then disaster struck; the poles were taken down and much of the brush cleared. We knew that there were few other nesting sites available and decided to test the idea that Elf Owls would use nest boxes. A graduate student began designing and predator-proofing boxes. Operating on a shoestring, we feared we would never be able to interest the birds in our accommodations, since we had neither the means nor the expertise for anything elaborate. We put up the first houses, on eight-foot fence posts with metal trash can predator guards, and laughed at the idea that any Elf Owl would be interested in making its home there. Two weeks later when we walked up to the post and tapped it, an angry little owl face emerged from the hole! Success! Today Elf Owls are frequently seen at Bentsen–Rio Grande Valley State Park, and development of the wildlife corridor along the Rio Grande River will surely improv

PAULINE JAMES,
as told to her student Leticia A. Alamía

© John P. ONeill - 1995

Ruby-throated Hummingbirds and Murray's Penstemon

Archilochus colubris and *Penstemon murrayanus*

ONE OF THE BEST-LOVED POEMS of Emily Dickinson begins:

A Route of Evanescence
With a revolving Wheel—
A Resonance of Emerald—
A Rush of Cochineal—
And every Blossom on the Bush
Adjusts its tumbled Head—

These few words give a true impression of the quickness, the blur of wings, and the flashes of green and red that characterize the Ruby-throated Hummingbird at a patch of flowers. To Emily Dickinson and to millions of us, this is *the* hummingbird. Although more than three hundred species of hummers inhabit the New World, eastern North America in the summertime belongs to the ruby-throat.

In the United States, the western edge of the ruby-throat's breeding range reaches East Texas. The Black-chinned Hummingbird, a common breeder in West Texas, is its closest relative. The two species are almost identical, so much so that in old black-and-white photos even the adult males are hard to tell apart.

Each March and April these far-flung members of a family of mainly tropical American birds leave their homes in Central America and head north. With the sudden flush of flowers and insects of the northern spring, the male birds arrive first and set up territories. The females soon follow and in a few weeks are building Lilliputian nests, laying eggs, and caring for their two young. Occasionally they have time to raise more than one brood, but in parts of Canada, where some hummers don't arrive until early June, their stay is notably brief. Before fall migration, ruby-throats add to their energy reserves by increasing their weight as much as 50 percent. From the southeastern

states, some birds evidently cross the Gulf of Mexico, flying nonstop for several hundred miles. Great numbers, however, fly south along the Gulf Coast of Texas, apparently taking the shortest overland route to Central America.

Inspired by this remarkable migration through coastal Texas, the Rockport area hosts a Hummer/Bird Celebration each September. In 1989, at the first festival, two hundred people attended lectures and went on field trips. Since then, the four-day event has grown rapidly. Now, several thousand visitors gather there each fall to say *adiós* to the hummingbirds until the following spring.

Near Corpus Christi, a retired lady once told me how she fed migrating hummers. One fall, larger numbers than usual passed through her yard, and for days she was kept busy mixing sugar water and carrying feeders in and out the back door. Her husband told her, "The doorknobs haven't been sticky like this since the kids were little!"

ERNEST FRANZGROTE

Black-chinned Hummingbirds and Red Buckeye

Archilochus alexandri and *Aesculus pavia*

BLACK-CHINNED HUMMINGBIRDS migrate north in March from the Pacific slope of Mexico, their purpose in Texas being to breed. During six months in Central and southwestern Texas, females raise two broods (where food supplies and predators permit), and adults and young then put on fat to fuel the first stage of the flight south. Suitable flowers, shady nest trees, and a dry climate partly define the black-chin's niche, and these elements can be found from the juniper-oak hills west of Austin to desert oases in Big Bend.

Breeding-season activities of males and females are very different. The sexes do not pair except to copulate, and a male provides no resources for females. Instead, he usually defends a territory of flowers, advertises his presence with display flights, and attempts to mate repeatedly. Females avoid nesting in or near male territories, for the price of doing so is constant harassment. Males display between March and June, the period when most eggs are laid. Probably a necessary prelude to mating, the displays also express aggression toward other males. One display involves power dives in a wide pendulum path, from a height of five to ten meters to near ground level and up again to the same height. There is a loud buzzing (from a burst of wingbeats) each time he reverses direction, and a whistle at the base of the dive (probably from air passing between sharply pointed tail feathers). A male who has a female interested or apparently trapped in brush may execute series of dives and close-range zigzags for fifteen minutes (including some rests). It appears to be an exhausting performance.

Because of the slow development of hummingbird eggs and young, successful breeding requires a two-month food supply. Small insects snapped during fly-catching bouts help meet protein needs, whereas sugars in nectar provide energy. A black-chin needs to burn about two grams of sugar to fuel a day of action and a night's sleep. Flowers that attract hummingbirds are hardly as rewarding as hummingbird feeders, typically producing only one to five milligrams of sugar daily. Given that an assortment of hummingbirds often harvest nectar from the same flower, the average rewards are often less than one milligram of sugar per flower, obliging the birds to make more than two thousand flower visits daily.

We know surprisingly little about which plants are important to black-chins. Probably fewer than 5 percent of Texas wildflowers produce enough nectar to turn a hummingbird into a faithful visitor; bees accept much smaller amounts or take pollen instead. Bluebonnets, for example, attract pollen-collecting bees, but because they produce no nectar, hummingbirds ignore them in favor of Indian paintbrush. Most wildflowers bloom for only two to three weeks, and birds use a sequence of species over the months, adjusting their home ranges as necessary. Although memory may help them to anticipate food-rich times and places, each year is somewhat different. Some Hill Country hummingbird foods include cedar sage, autumn sage, cut-leaf penstemon, claret-cup cactus, anisacanthus, and turk's cap. In addition, there are probably a few dozen Texas nectar plants unknown in hummingbird natural history annals but not unknown to this bird.

PETER SCOTT

64

Blue-throated Hummingbird and Claret Cup Cactus

Lampornis clemenciae and *Echinocereus triglochidiatus*

THE LOUD, continuous *seep seep seep* of a male Blue-throated Hummingbird dominated the canyon. I searched the high foliage of an Arizona cypress, trying to find the perpetrator, without success. Its loud song continued. Finally, I moved a short distance up the slope behind me, above the heavily wooded canyon to where I could see the top of the high cypress. There it was, sitting in the open at the very top, proclaiming to all the world, especially to any other blue-throated males that might be in the area, that it was "king of the hill."

I could clearly see its bright-blue throat, gleaming iridescent in the morning light. Through binoculars, I also could see its two white facial stripes and, when it shifted position, its black tail with bold white corner patches. The contrasting tail helps to separate this hummer from the Magnificent Hummingbird, the other large hummer that occurs in the Chisos Mountains. Although female blue-throats lack the blue throat of the male, they do possess the bold tail patches, though in gray. Both of these large hummers reach the northern edge of their breeding range in West Texas, as well as in the mountains of southeastern Arizona, the northern extension of Mexico's Sierra Madre Oriental and Occidental, respectively.

I wondered if my blue-throat's mate was sitting on a well-hidden nest, constructed of moss and plant fibers and bound together with spider webbing and plant down, somewhere on the huge cypress.

The male Blue-throated Hummingbird suddenly took wing, diving down in hot pursuit of a passing Broad-tailed Hummingbird that, apparently, had unknowingly invaded its territory. I could hear the blue-throat's constant *seep* notes for a surprising distance as it pursued the smaller hummingbird down Boot Canyon. Only then did I detect other songbirds in the area. Bewick's Wren and Tufted (Black-crested) Titmouse, Ash-throated Flycatcher, Hepatic Tanager, and Scott's Oriole were singing from the higher pinyon-and-juniper-covered slopes; a troupe of Mexican Jays called from the oaks up-canyon; and at least three Colima Warblers were singing among the oaks and maples in the canyon bottom. And from further down the canyon drifted the faint song of a Painted Redstart.

An Acorn Woodpecker suddenly flew to the cypress top, perched in the open, and called several loud *ja-cob* notes. Just as suddenly, it dashed out in pursuit of a passing insect, which it captured in midair. As it flew back to the cypress, the male blue-throat returned. And, in spite of the great size difference, it attacked the much larger woodpecker, which immediately flew off to find a perch elsewhere. Seconds later, after only a halfhearted pursuit, the blue-throat returned to its high perch. It preened its feathers for a few seconds and then commenced singing: *seep seep seep.*

ROLAND "RO" WAUER

Green Kingfisher, Maximilian Sunflower, and Sycamore

Chloroceryle americana, Helianthus maximilianii, and *Platanus occidentalis*

AS ONE WALKS ALONG the Rio Grande or a stream in the southern half of the Hill Country or the South Texas brushlands, a flash of iridescent green indicates the presence of the Green Kingfisher, a species widespread throughout tropical America. Unlike its larger cousin, the Belted Kingfisher, which is found across Texas, the Green Kingfisher will more likely be *seen* than *heard.* And in contrast to the Belted and Ringed Kingfishers, the male of this diminutive bird has the brighter plumage, including the dark-orange "belt" on the breast. As in many birds, the young tend to resemble the female, but they have a suffusion of light buff across the breast and some spotting on the upper breast.

When not streaking up or down a watercourse, the Green Kingfisher often sits on a branch that extends over the water. There it patiently waits, watching for a fish to approach in the water. Down it dives, into the water; if successful, it often returns to its perch to consume the fish. Or, if the bird has young, it may return to its nest burrow to feed them. The burrow is usually located just below the top of the stream bank, perhaps at a bend in the stream or under an overhang. Once the young have fledged, the family group will range several hundred yards up and down the stream, while the parents attempt to find enough fish to satisfy the appetites of their young. If the grown-ups don't produce the fish at a sufficiently brisk rate, one or more fledglings will pursue a parent along the stream, calling persistently.

While Texas claims a number of tropical birds as part of its avifauna, especially in the lower Rio Grande Valley, none provides quite the thrill for me as does this jewel. To me, the Green Kingfisher *is* South Texas!

KEITH ARNOLD

Golden-fronted Woodpeckers and Texas Oak

Melanerpes aurifrons and *Quercus buckleyi*

GOLDEN-FRONTED WOODPECKERS are not shy birds. I admire their engaging personalities. They come readily to bird feeders filled with sunflower seeds. They also have a penchant for fruit (especially oranges), berries, nuts, mixtures of suet and peanut butter, and insects.

I often see them at suet-and-peanut-butter logs and orange halves that look as if they are sprouting from trees in the Texas Rio Grande Valley and on the Edwards Plateau. Kay McCracken, author of *Birding South Texas,* describes golden-fronts as "pampered and spoiled," because campers in some of the parks in South Texas put orange halves on mesquite and hackberry trees especially for them.

I have a friend in Concan, Texas, who enjoys spoiling them. One male Golden-fronted Woodpecker that she nicknamed "Fussbudget" likes the peanut butter treat that she provides for him, but he wants it on a certain limb of the tree near her back door. She smears it on a limb and then calls him by name, "Here, Fussbudget! Here, Fussbudget!" When he hears her voice, he stops whatever he is doing and flies roller-coaster fashion from across the Frio River to her clifftop home. When she places the peanut butter on his favorite limb, he obliges her by gobbling it down. If she tries a new location, he ignores it and returns to his business across the river, but not before he scolds her soundly.

Both male and female golden-fronts excavate their nest cavity in limbs that may be dead or alive, and both parents attend the young. Their range reaches from extreme southwestern Oklahoma throughout the midsection of Texas to Nicaragua. I have observed nesting golden-fronts on both sides of the Mexican border. Once while tromping through a Tamaulipan Thorn Forest a few miles south of the Rio Grande, I heard the hungry cries of golden-front nestlings coming from a cavity in a mesquite tree. It wasn't long before one of the attentive parents came to fill the gaping mouths. After the parent departed, I placed my small tape recorder near the nest hole to record the nestlings' cries.

Three curious Tamaulipan schoolchildren happened by on their way home for lunch and wondered what I was doing. I pointed out the nest hole to them and played the recording after showing them the bird's picture in the field guide. Of course they recognized the vividly colored woodpecker, since it lives near their home.

My Mexican guide and interpreter, Patin, explained to the children that I was in their country to study the birds of the area. He told them how important it is to protect nesting sites such as this; then I recorded and played back each of their voices when they told us their names. As they listened I saw a hint of wonder in their bright, sparkling eyes.

I think hearing the Golden-fronted Woodpecker nestlings, as well as hearing their own voices for the first time, made a lasting impression on Ramón, Yolanda, and Emilio. I know I shall long remember sharing the high-spirited bird with three beautiful children whose language I do not speak or understand.

JUNE OSBORNE

© John P. O'Neill - 1993

Scissor-tailed Flycatcher and Texas Bluebonnets

Tyrannus forficatus and *Lupinus texensis*

THE SCISSOR-TAILED FLYCATCHER is the Oklahoma state bird, a fact I knew when I was growing up in Oklahoma, although I rarely saw the bird until we moved to Texas, where it is found in nearly every county. It was the first bird I cared about. I often noticed them nesting on the tops of telephone poles or decorating the fence lines along Texas highways, their long tails hanging down like quarter notes on a musical staff.

The scissortail seems to enjoy being noticed, which made it easier for a young bird watcher to appreciate its qualities. Gray birds rarely catch our eye, but the grayness of the scissortail is soft and luminous, like a cloud with the sun behind it. The sides and underparts are splashed in a color that ranges from scarlet to a creamy orange that I associate with Dreamsicles. The great, forked, black-and-white tail is twice the length of the body. It appears cumbersome and mainly ornamental in repose—a little too much, to be honest about it. There is a tiny thunderbolt of scarlet in the crown, rarely seen unless the scissortail flares at a crow or hawk intruding into its territory. It is wonderful to observe the fierce little warrior harrying the larger bird, like an acrobatic fighter jet flying circles around a lumbering bomber.

We call it a flycatcher, but it tends to feed on grasshoppers and beetles, often plucking them off the ground, which seems like poor sport for such an agile critter. When some airborne morsel floats into view, the scissortail rockets up and then flashes open that amazing tail, which seems to give it purchase on the air—it freezes, spread-eagled. Such beauty, one gasps. In courtship, the male goes plumb crazy, zigzagging and somersaulting and cutting long, swooning rollover loops in the air, all the while making his characteristic *keck-keck-keck* cackling call.

In my youth, the scissortail was abundant everywhere in Texas; now this beloved bird is noticeably reduced in numbers. The once-great flocks of scissortails that migrated to Mexico and Central America in the fall are severely diminished. Perhaps this has happened because of fire ants, which have done such insufferable damage to the variety and abundance of Texas birdlife by destroying the insects they feed on; perhaps it is a result of the overuse of pesticides in Central America. It is an awful loss.

LAWRENCE WRIGHT

72

© John R. O'Neill · 1984

Vermilion Flycatchers and Mesquite *Pyrocephalus rubinus* and *Prosopis glandulosa*

WE STILL RECALL VIVIDLY the first time we witnessed the courtship flight of the Vermilion Flycatcher. Perched on an acacia branch beside a quiet pond in deep South Texas, the male suddenly launched into flight and climbed in sweeping circles high in the air, all the time singing a soft, tinkling song. At the top of his towering rise, he hung on fluttering wings like a giant butterfly, his erect crown feathers gleaming in the sun, his tail cocked upward and spread. Puffing out his vermilion chest, he continued to sing as he hung suspended, then abruptly fluttered down again to land on a branch beside his chosen mate.

We presume the female flycatcher was suitably impressed; we were filled with awe. Since that first memorable meeting, we have seen countless Vermilion Flycatchers and watched many such courtship displays. Each is a special gift, an avian treat of which we never tire.

"But surely only the phlegmatic person, professional or amateur, can see the vermilion flycatcher for the first time without a gasp of surprise and pleasure," wrote Roy Bedichek in his classic *Adventures with a Texas Naturalist.* Indeed, few birds can equal its surprising beauty, especially in a family that routinely cloaks its members in somber shades.

The male's dark, sooty-brown back, wings, and tail contrast sharply with the flaming red of its crown and underparts. The genus name, *Pyrocephalus,* means "fire-headed" in Greek, while the specific epithet, *rubinus,* is Latin for "ruby red." Equally descriptive is one of several Spanish names for this six-inch flycatcher: *brasita de fuego,* or "little coal of fire." Certainly a flame seems to burn deep within, for the Vermilion Flycatcher's plumage glows too brightly to be mere pigmented color.

The female, though much less colorful, is charming nonetheless. Her upperparts are grayish brown with a darker tail; her pale underparts are streaked with dusky gray and flushed with salmon pink. More suitably camouflaged than her mate, the female incubates alone on her nest of twigs carefully lined with soft grasses, plant fibers, and feathers. Her two to four white eggs are blotched with brown and lilac. The flamboyant male feeds her through the two-week incubation and helps care for the young until they fledge.

The Vermilion Flycatcher ranges from the southwestern United States through Central and South America to southern Argentina. It nests in the western portions of Texas southward to the Rio Grande and wanders widely in winter to other sections of the state. Preferring thickets and woodland edges near small ponds, it frequently perches on shrubs and fences beside the water and darts out to capture flying insects in midair. Each sortie by the male brings enormous pleasure even to veteran observers, for few birds surpass the elegance of the flaming "little coal of fire."

JOHN AND GLORIA TVETEN

Cave Swallows *Petrochelidon fulva*

CREATURES OF SUNLIGHT, creatures of the open air, swallows are the last birds that we might imagine dwelling underground. But one swallow is famed, and named, for its habit of nesting in caves.

For many years, Cave Swallows north of the Mexican border were practically limited to Texas, frequenting certain caves and sinkholes in the Hill Country. Going to see them was something of an adventure: getting directions, getting permission from landowners, then making a long, dusty, tooth-jarring drive, followed by a hike across rough country to the caves. Not into the caves, mind you. We would sit outside to watch the birds coming and going. The swallows used the caves only as shelter for raising their young, and they went no farther inside than the last filtering of light. At the twilight edge of darkness, the swallows would plaster mud against the rock walls to build the nests in which they would lay their eggs and feed their young. Not until the baby Cave Swallows were big enough to fly would they emerge, blinking, into the sunlight.

But the birders were the ones who were left blinking, in surprise, when the Cave Swallows emerged en masse from the caves in the 1970s.

Many of us experienced the same revelation, while driving a Texas highway in the spring: suddenly thinking, *Wait a minute—what were those birds?* and going back to find a little flock of Cave Swallows swirling in and out of a culvert, or around a bridge. Apparently pioneering swallows had discovered that culverts were like mini-caves, except far more abundant, and that the spaces under bridges were somewhat like caves—close enough, anyway. No longer limited by the scarcity of natural nest sites, Cave Swallows exploded in number. Leapfrogging along the highways as they established new colonies, they spread west to El Paso, south to the Rio Grande, east almost to the Louisiana line, as if they meant to embrace all of Texas. The bird that once had been an elusive specialty was now a common roadside sight.

But of course they did not all move into modern sites. Some Cave Swallows remained in their ancestral haunts, and not long ago, some friends and I went back to one of these places, a cave in the Hill Country north of Uvalde.

We arrived late in the day. The cave entrance, half hidden behind scrubby oaks on the hillside, was dark and mysterious, but everything else in the scene was bathed in evening sun. The colors of the Cave Swallows looked rich and bright in that low-angled light, deep buff and chestnut and slaty blue, as the birds circled and swooped over the hills. Their soft, liquid call notes echoed as they darted in and out of the cavern's mouth.

As the sun slipped behind the western ridges, the swallows milled about, seemingly torn with indecision: whether to make one more foraging flight or take to the security of the cave for the night. It seemed as if they anticipated something happening. Apparently they did. Before the last of the swallows had entered the cave, a muffled whirring or rustling sound grew out of the depths, and the first wave of bats came pouring out into the evening sky.

We had come, in fact, mostly to watch the evening exodus of bats. Like the Cave Swallows, the Mexican free-tailed bats used this cave as a place to raise their young. Like the swallows, they caught flying insects in the air over the surrounding country. But they did their hunting at night, and they also differed in numbers: at this cave, at least, the bats were vastly more abundant. Tens of thousands of them, perhaps hundreds of thousands, would spread out from this point across hundreds of square miles, to scoop beetles and moths out of the air until dawn brought them home to roost again.

We watched as the sky grew darker, while the stream of bats coming out of the cave swelled to a torrent, with thousands pouring out every minute, to swirl away in a long, twisting plume into the distance. They were still coming when it was too dark to see. As we turned to leave we could hear the voices of Cave Swallows that had not yet entered the cave, now temporarily creatures of the darkness after all, circling and calling somewhere overhead against the stars.

KENN KAUFMAN

Blue Jay and Japanese Magnolia

Cyanocitta cristata and *Magnolia soulangiana* hybrid

AMBIVALENCE is not an applicable word when people consider the Blue Jay; everyone has a definite opinion of this distinctive bird. Almost from their first acquaintance with the jay, humans employ a diverse range of adjectives trying to define, judge, and characterize it. Early ornithologists decried its fondness for the eggs and nestlings of other birds and the occasional thievery of domestic fruit and grain as proof of its evil nature, although its omnivorous appetite is no more than a minor copy of our own. The Blue Jay's varied taste includes acorns and other nuts, which it habitually carries off and caches for future use. Buried in various locations, these fruits are retrieved, abandoned, or forgotten, depending on need. Those left unused frequently germinate. Thus we have in the Blue Jay an invaluable forester.

The Blue Jay is intelligent, inquisitive, and interesting enough to have been celebrated in the writings of authors as diverse as Mark Twain, e.e. cummings, and Henry David Thoreau. That they selected this fascinating creature should come as no surprise. Everything jays do is carried out with élan. Watch a Blue Jay moving about a tree. It doesn't hop, it bounces from limb to limb, as if it were made of rubber, until it has reached its goal or has launched itself into the air. In springtime, jays frequently indulge in a game of chase that generally involves several males in pursuit of some covetable female. Then the limb-bouncing becomes even more pronounced, and the lady and her ensemble of suitors move from tree to tree until she makes her choice.

Even though the Blue Jay is classed as a songbird, many might denigrate its voice, since it is known more for its distinctively raucous noisemaking than anything else. A jay that happens upon a drowsing owl, a snake, or a human hunter declares the impending danger with such a clamor that every creature within earshot is alerted and nearby jays flock to the aid of the discoverer, adding their own indignant remarks. That, however, is not the limit of their vocalizations. Though few people would believe that Blue Jays can actually sing, they can and do. Called a whisper song, seldom heard by humans, it is delivered quietly and seems to be performed solely for the benefit of the singer. It is soft, sweet, and charming. Then, too, the jay can mimic and frequently imitates the call of the Red-shouldered Hawk to perfection.

The name Blue Jay is rather inadequate for this dandy; it deserves a richer title. Nearly all the world's jays are blue to some degree. Our subject is actually plumaged in a wide variety of bluish tints, the most prominent of which is cerulean. Hence, Cerulean Jay. It also sports black piping around the face—Bridled Jay, perhaps? Whatever the name, one cannot deny the superlative beauty of the rascal. Crested, blued, and enhanced with black and white, it is indisputably one of the most handsome of the corvid clan. If it were rare and restricted to some remote mountaintop, bird watchers would seek it out as a great avian prize. Blue Jays may be common but they are no less beautiful for that. Our small planet is a richer place because we share it with jays, and the Blue Jay deserves acceptance as one of our greatest treasures.

BEN FELTNER

Green Jays and Huisache *Cyanocorax yncas* and *Acacia farnesiana*

I SAW MY FIRST GREEN JAY as a bird-crazy fourth grader in 1954. This blessed event took place on the El Sauz Ranch in Willacy County, barely within the range of the species, at the northern edge of the lower Rio Grande Valley, known then, as now, simply as the Valley. At the time my uncle, who worked for Humble Oil (now Exxon), lived in the "Humble Camp," a small tract of homes for oil company employees on the giant ranch. I lived with my family about eighty miles north, in Kingsville.

The El Sauz Ranch was a magic place to me. How could there be so many great and unfamiliar birds scarcely an hour and a half from Kingsville? The jays were only the tip of the iceberg, and on that first trip and subsequent ones I marveled at Hooded and Audubon's Orioles, Great Kiskadees, Plain Chachalacas. Miraculously, I even worked out the identity of the tiny Northern Beardless Tyrannulet with the help of my well-thumbed first edition of Roger Tory Peterson's *Field Guide to Western Birds*.

On the frontispiece of this classic was a beautiful color plate featuring the jays and other species. Peterson depicted most of the jays with beaks open, scolding loudly, no doubt, a trait for which the group is well known. I soon learned that despite the raucous *cheg, che-che-che-che* scolding bouts in which Green Jays engage when they discover a slinking bobcat or a big western diamondback, these birds are actually rather shy and elusive, especially when compared to the Blue Jay, a real "jay's jay" by anyone's standard.

The common view I had of these magnificent birds (and I pursued them endlessly) was a flash of green and yellow, the latter from the outer feathers of the tail, as they slipped away into the thorny brush. The flared yellow-and-green tail of the Green Jay, such an unusual color pattern even for a tropical bird, was the inspiration for the knitted wool cap faithfully worn by Edgar Kincaid, patron saint of Texas birds and birders, on all the numerous National Audubon Society Christmas Bird Counts that he conducted in Green Jay country over the years. The "Green Jay Flying Away" cap (knitted by Suzanne Winckler) was worn to honor this marvelous creature in its habitat, just as ships fly the host nation's colors whenever they are in one of its ports.

The Green Jay's empire in Texas has become considerably larger since my days in the 1950s. The species is just one of a number of "Valley birds" (e.g., Great Kiskadee, Couch's Kingbird, Ringed Kingfisher) that have pushed their ranges steadily northward across South Texas, literally to the limits of the region at the foot of the Balcones Escarpment. This spread northward by Green Jays and other tropical species has been explained as the consequence of global warming or as the result of natural range expansion and contraction, although no one can say for certain why it is taking place.

Like most jays, Green Jays are highly social creatures. After the breeding season, the birds form bands of four to ten individuals and roam widely. These are probably family groups, perhaps composed of a pair of breeding adults and their offspring from the last breeding season or two. It is the wanderings of bands at this season that takes birds out of their "normal" range. A wandering group of Green Jays that finds suitable habitat may well settle and remain to breed the following season. This is what seems to be happening in places like Del Rio, Brackettville, and the Coastal Bend. Fairly conspicuous in the nonbreeding season and most likely to be seen in towns and around other areas frequented by humans at that time, Green Jays seem to do a disappearing act when they are actively breeding, becoming very quiet and furtive. In fact, I can count on one hand the number of active nests that I have found in more than forty years of birding.

Despite the toll taken by cowbird parasitism, there is no doubt that the Green Jay is doing quite well in Texas. It now occurs over approximately the southern one-fifth of the state, and its total population has probably increased by an order of magnitude since I first made its acquaintance in the mesquite and live oak woodlands of the El Sauz Ranch.

In a world where success stories among wild creatures are not common, it is comforting that one of our most spectacular and interesting birds is not only holding its own but seems to be thriving. During a long career of leading bird-watching tours in South Texas and other parts of the world, I would invariably be asked at the beginning of a tour, "Do we have a chance of seeing Green Jays?" With a serious look I would always answer, "Well, we're certainly going to give it our best try." Deep inside I had a broad, satisfied smile.

JOHN ARVIN

Northern Mockingbird and Yaupon Holly *Mimus polyglottos* and *Ilex vomitoria*

A SPRINGTIME SATURDAY, 5 A.M. For most folks, a good time to be sleeping. But for teenaged naturalists growing up in Houston, it was time to go birding. With field gear and breakfast packed the night before, we'd tiptoe out the driveway door, trying our best not to disturb the sleeping household. But we never escaped detection. Trusty as any watchdog, the mockingbird that ruled the row of holly trees by our drive was alert to the creak of a door, the least glimmer of light, or the clunk of gear in the car trunk. Unseen but not unseeing, he would issue forth his liquid voice from the holly gloom, bold and strong, challenging any disturbance to the peace of his realm.

These lovely nocturnes were thrilling to me, forming seductive preludes to other avian wonders that we might encounter in those days afield. They form my most vivid memories of the mockingbird. I have spent many happy days with family and friends wandering the verdant marshes, beaches, and coastal woods that fringe the Texas coast, always looking for one more bird in this most bird-rich region of the United States. Often, the mockingbird in the holly trees was the first and last bird of the day, announcing its vigilance as we left before dawn, celebrating its primacy when we returned after dark.

The propensity to sing at night is not the only remarkable quality of the mockingbird. It is often judged to be one of the finest singers among North American birds. It sings year-round, usually from prominent perches on top of bushes, trees, fences, or power lines. Its ability to imitate other birds, from which its name is derived, is amazing at times. Individual mockers may incorporate the songs of more than fifty birds in their repertoires. This tendency toward mimicry is most pronounced in the northern part of its range but is still well known in Texas. Sometimes other birds' songs are copied directly. At other times, single notes or phrases from another species are incorporated into a medley of song, much of which is original with the mocker.

Though its black, white, and gray tones might be thought somber by some, I have always felt that the mockingbird's plumage is distinctive and well suited to the businesslike character of the bird. Its amber eyes give it an alert look that goes with its engaged, often vigilant behavior. With its broad wings and ample tail, flight can be slow and splashy or deft and maneuverable, as circumstances dictate. Bright patches of white in the wings and tail are hidden when the bird is at rest but flash suddenly when it takes to flight. The white wing patches are prominent in a peculiar, stereotyped behavior that mockingbirds perform while foraging. From an erect stance on the ground, the bird takes a short run forward. It then raises its wings deliberately out to the side and over its head, with one or two mechanical pauses along the way. It holds this "wings up" position for a second or two before snapping the wings closed, running forward again, and repeating the sequence. It may do so three or four times in succession. This curious display may increase foraging efficiency by flushing prey items.

The mockingbird is one of the few native species well adapted to life in the urban and suburban landscape. Mockers forage boldly on lawns, in gardens, and in hedgerows. From early spring through late summer, they vigorously defend their breeding territory from other mockers and potential predators, such as cats, dogs, hawks, owls, and crows. Many a surprised house cat in the vicinity of a mockingbird's nest has had to turn tail and run from the righteous onslaught of the inhabitant. Their lively songs and acrobatic antics make them especially conspicuous as they go about their daily lives. Though ubiquitous in open and edge habitats throughout the South and Southwest, mocking-birds reach their greatest abundance in the dense brush country of South Texas and the western Edwards Plateau. Together, these features make them one of the most familiar and best-loved birds of Texas. They truly deserve their status as the official state bird.

MICHAEL BRAUN

Curve-billed Thrasher and Texas Prickly Pear

Toxostoma curvirostre and *Opuntia engelmannii* var. *texana*

I CAN'T RECALL THE DATE of seeing my first Curve-billed Thrasher, but I do remember my first trip to see "brush-country" birds on the Caron Ranch in McMullen County with good friends Nancy and Jerry Strickling and high school buddy Ralph Peterson. It was in the spring, probably in 1957 or 1958, and it must have been in April, as I can remember the overwhelming, almost sickening, perfume of one of those spectacular South Texas blooms that follows a wet fall and winter. In a station wagon full of food and accompanied by an eager entourage of other Houston-area birders, we made our way west of George West along Ranch Road 1962, stopping at regular intervals to see a myriad of bird species that simply did not exist on the upper Gulf coastal plain.

I have always been prone to go off by myself so that no one would interfere with my bird watching, and the fact that the property in the area was not fenced made it simple to silently slip away with only a few steps off the dirt road. I wandered down a small draw, found a place to hide under a dense catclaw, and stopped to squeak. In only a few seconds I was almost hit in the face by a large bird that rocketed into the bush and let out an explosive *who-whooit*. Right in front of me was a large grayish thrasher with an incredible brilliant orange eye. One slight movement to try to bring my binoculars to my face and the bird dropped, let out several more *who-whooit* calls, and was engulfed by the brush. That is the type of experience that joins bird and birder for life—it is over in an instant but never forgotten! To this day I am always drawn straight to the eye when I see a Curve-billed Thrasher. We would see many more of these wonderful birds that weekend, as well as other "lifers" such as Pyrrhuloxias, Verdins, Cactus Wrens, and even a seemingly lost migrant male Black-throated Green Warbler that was feeding in scrubby willows at a small cattle tank. After hearing the thrashers over several days, we decided that they sounded like someone hailing a taxi, so we dubbed them the "taxicab bird." I have now seen Curve-billed Thrashers in four states and in Mexico, and each time I am transported back to that initial experience in South Texas, always wondering why there is such a demand for taxis when there isn't even a road!

Most of the paintings in this book bring together a bird and a plant, and often a particular place, at least in my mind. Although I had previously seen the orange variant of the Texas prickly pear cactus, which most often has yellow flowers, when I reencountered it, blooming profusely, in Atascosa County several years ago, it became inevitable that I would have to paint that plant with the Curve-billed Thrasher. Although thrashers do use the cactus for feeding and nesting, it was the orange eye, which so exactly matches the delicate cactus flowers and so perfectly combines a brilliant splash of spring color with the soft grays of the bird, that moved me to put them together.

I have gone on to study mostly tropical birds, but those early experiences with Texas birds and friends are ever present and remain among the richest of my life. I also still find the brush country of South Texas one of the most exciting and interesting habitats anywhere. The late Jerry Strickling always ended a birding trek with the question "What's the best bird of the trip?" My immediate answer would be "the Curve-billed Thrasher, of course!"

JOHN P. O'NEILL

Wood Thrush and American Beautyberry

Hylocichla mustelina and *Callicarpa americana*

I CANNOT IMAGINE a spring morning without the song of the Wood Thrush. The call haunts my childhood memories as does no other sound. For me, spring has not arrived until I am awakened by the Wood Thrush. Its clarion, flutelike melodies still give me goose bumps, first in the dream state of preconsciousness and then in the full realization that winter has finally passed, and, in the words of Solomon's Song, "the time of singing has come." No other bird song on earth produces such emotion in me.

As a migrant, the Wood Thrush can be seen and heard throughout the eastern half of Texas in April and May. After that, it is still a fairly common nesting bird of the East Texas woodlands. If you draw a line from Dallas southeast to Huntsville and on to Houston, you define the western edge of its breeding range. From there, its range extends eastward along the Gulf Coast and the northern border of Florida to the Atlantic Ocean, northward from Texas to South Dakota, and then eastward through the eastern states and the southern extremes of Ontario and Quebec to the southern tip of Maine.

The Wood Thrush's winter quarters extend from Mexico to Panama. It is silent there, and consequently there is little to draw attention to its eminence amid all the raucous sounds and brilliant colors of its tropical avian neighbors. On rare occasions, a Wood Thrush will spend the winter in the subtropical areas of the United States. I once had the privilege of finding one of the very few Wood Thrushes ever to be listed on an annual Christmas Bird Count. There it was, running robinlike along the leaf-strewn ground under the palms and live oaks beside a canal. It looked very out of place in that habitat. And it didn't utter a sound. But its rusty head, fawn-colored back, and heavily spotted breast were unmistakable. Perhaps for the first time in my life, I realized that the Wood Thrush had an artistic quality in addition to its beautiful song.

But all is not well in the deep woods where this phantom bird calls. Because of fragmentation, if not outright destruction, of necessary forests in the Wood Thrush's wintering and breeding ranges, the future of this delightful denizen of the deep woods is in doubt. In its tropical range, the thrush's natural environment is being cleared to provide for increasing human populations. In its breeding range, the threat is more subtle.

Brown-headed Cowbirds, with the aid of humans, are devastating the Wood Thrush population in the United States. Recent research in the forests of the eastern United States has shown that in order to breed successfully, a pair of Wood Thrushes requires at least a forty-acre expanse of uninterrupted forest. When the deep woods are altered by something as seemingly minor as a logging road or an occasional clearing, the Brown-headed Cowbird moves in and disturbs the life cycle of the Wood Thrush. The cowbird, a species of open country and clearings, always lays its eggs in the nests of other birds, and thus its predation on young thrushes is insidious. In such a disturbed environment, the adult thrushes unwittingly feed and rear the young cowbirds at the expense of their own young. Like the blackbirds of Tolkien's trilogy, the cowbirds are taking the kingdom.

It is almost impossible to conceive of the silent spring that Rachel Carson predicted. But that possibility exists if we do not preserve a sufficient amount of deep woods where the Wood Thrush, among other birds, can continue to thrill future generations with its transcendent song. I have always said that if I had to lose my sight or my hearing, I would rather lose my sight. The Wood Thrush has a lot to do with that.

JAMES A. TUCKER

Eastern Bluebirds and Flowering Dogwood *Sialia sialis* and *Cornus florida*

I FIRST MADE MY ACQUAINTANCE with the Eastern Bluebird on a gray November day when I was thirteen years old and had been invited along on a special field trip with the San Antonio Audubon Society. We were in the heavy brush along the Medina River on a morning after a heavy rainstorm, and there was a magical fallout of arriving migratory birds, all of them new to me—House Wrens, Ruby-crowned Kinglets, Orange-crowned Warblers, and Lincoln's Sparrows.

Suddenly the trip leader looked up and pointed out a flock of small birds flying southward, riding the cold front. "Bluebirds, the first bluebirds!" They were small, dull shapes in a loose flock, and then they were gone, a disappointment to me. "How did she even know what they were?" I wondered. So I asked, and she said, "The soft call notes." They were notes that only the most attentive and experienced ear could pick out.

Such things make an impression on a boy from New York City, one just awakening to the wonder of the birds all around him in his new home in the wilds of Texas. I became a regular on the field trips, and it wasn't long before I finally saw the Eastern Bluebird as it should be seen, in full, glorious color on a brisk winter day, enlivening the oaks and dark junipers of the Hill Country, gathering in small flocks along the wires, dropping to the ground for insects and fluttering into the trees for berries.

I have now lived in East Texas for more than twenty-five years. Nowhere in the world is the Eastern Bluebird more abundant than here in the Piney Woods. The soft and lovely song of the male is one of the first harbingers of spring, and when I hear it on a warm February morning I know it is time to clean the nest boxes, for the males will shortly begin checking for nest sites. Logging and farming practices throughout the region favor the bluebird, leaving an abundance of woodlots and trees, snags, old wooden fences, abandoned wood houses, and clear-cuts. Though the habitat we have now is a far cry from the original pine savannah that blanketed East Texas, the bluebird finds the alterations quite acceptable, full of food sources and potential nest sites.

From March until late summer it seems that the bluebirds are constantly busy, barely getting one brood raised before starting on the next, endlessly carrying food to hungry youngsters. Amid the heavy greenery of summer this brilliant flash of blue is still present along the roadsides, but with the first cooler and drier days the birds become inconspicuous, taking a much-needed rest while molting. Then, as the autumn cold fronts become stronger and more frequent, the small groups form along the country lanes again. By late November bluebirds begin arriving from the north to augment the resident population. Teaming up with robins, Pine Warblers, and Chipping Sparrows to form loose flocks that throng through the open pines and roadsides, bluebirds enhance every winter day. On the few days that are bitterly cold, the bluebirds and their companions retreat to the cover of the river bottoms to find shelter in the crowns of the dense hardwoods.

I have long participated in the Audubon Christmas Bird Count, and it pleases me to know that the region where I live typically has the highest concentrations of Eastern Bluebirds recorded. For more than twenty years now I have led birding tours far and wide, seeking out rare and exotic birds all over the world and sharing them with others, but I know none that is more beautiful than our bluebird. Its colorful presence and gentle demeanor bring year-round joy to all who love this pleasant countryside, providing for me a familiar and abiding link to the place I call home.

DAVID E. WOLF

©John P. O'Neill · 1984

Black-capped Vireos and Mohr Oak *Vireo atricapillus* and *Quercus mohriana*

THE MILITARY EXPLORATION of Texas was in full force by the mid-nineteenth century. Army topographical engineers were surveying possible routes for a railroad to the Pacific, and the United States and Mexico boundary line was in need of clear demarcation. In addition to their primary survey tasks, field parties were under an official mandate to document natural resources. Among the scientists accompanying survey teams were physician naturalists and zoological and botanical collectors.

In conjunction with these efforts, on May 26, 1851, Dr. S. W. Woodhouse collected two specimens of an unknown songbird along the Devils (then San Pedro) River near present-day Juno. He was attracted to the bird's singular song and its active, warblerlike behavior. The following year Woodhouse formally described and named *Vireo atricapillus*. The Black-capped Vireo was one of the last vireo species described from the United States, and to scientists it was one of the oddest. In only this, the near-smallest of the vireos, are the sexes notably different in plumage.

Understanding of the black-cap's distribution was slow to materialize. It was first reported to the east along the Balcones Escarpment of the Edwards Plateau in 1879 and then at its historical northern extent in south central Kansas in 1885. By the turn of the century, the breeding range was known to extend from Kansas through central Oklahoma into Central Texas and then west and south into Coahuila, Mexico. Although still poorly known, its winter range lies on the Pacific slope of Mexico, largely in Sinaloa and Nayarit. Certainly, the black-cap is one of the most restricted of temperate-breeding North American birds.

Contributing to its mystery, its life history was little known until 1957. Since then, efforts to understand it have intensified, unfortunately in response to its sharp decline in range and abundance in the United States. The Black-capped Vireo is, at the time of this writing, an officially endangered species. It now is absent in Kansas, barely holding on in Oklahoma, and greatly reduced in the eastern portion of its Texas range.

The diminutive migrant returns to Texas each spring in late March and April and leaves by mid-September. A pair occupies about two to four acres of shrubby terrain, in which the nest is built a few feet off the ground in the densest foliage. Although the clutch size is three to four eggs and the pairs may attempt to nest as many as six times a season, black-caps produce too few young. Among other problems, they suffer alarming rates of cowbird parasitism (up to 90 percent of nests).

Finding potential Black-capped Vireo habitat can be easy, although seeing the bird is often a challenge. The species is a classic habitat specialist. Within its general range, in the ecotone between plains or desert grassland and forest, black-caps select deciduous shrubbery. Among the peculiar vegetational features apparently demanded by this vireo are dense deciduous foliage to ground level and open spaces between bushes. Here in Texas, shin oaks, scrub oaks, and sumacs most often fit the requirements where they occur in thicketlike patches on the thin, rocky soil of eroded slopes, gullies, and ravine edges. It can be easy to walk through Black-capped Vireo habitat, but not in a straight line. One is forced to meander back and forth, following the open spaces around nearly impenetrable patches of shrubbery.

Getting a good look at this striking bird can be maddening. The male's complicated and melodious song easily announces its presence from several layers of oak shrubbery. It most often remains within the foliage, presenting only brief glimpses of its shadowy form. Lucky is the novice birder who clearly sees the jet-black cap, white spectacles, and red eyes of this most distinctively patterned of North American vireos.

In my Concho Valley region of Texas, the Black-capped Vireo is a link with the past. Irish immigrant William Lloyd first wrote of it here in 1884. His brief report on finding it really was not rich with new knowledge of the species, but nonetheless, it was the earliest account in a scientific journal of a bird species at my home. When, ninety years later, I established my doctoral study of the Concho Valley bird fauna, the selection of my scrub oak census plot had much to do with Lloyd and the vireo. I chose a study site that was most likely to be near the location of Lloyd's discovery. Black-capped Vireos were there for Lloyd, there for me, and I hope will be there for others in the twenty-first century.

TERRY C. MAXWELL

© John P. O'Neill · 1986

Golden-cheeked Warblers and Ashe Juniper

Dendroica chrysoparia and *Juniperus ashei*

WHILE MUCH OF THE COUNTRY might pay homage to the first robin seen in the yard as the harbinger of spring, nothing signals the season so stirringly for bird watchers in Central Texas as the arrival of the first Golden-cheeked Warbler. Others might be so academic as to take note of the date of the vernal equinox or wait to start their gardens after the average date of the last freeze, but for us, it's spring when the golden-cheeks show up, on or about March 10.

Not that all of Mother Nature's realm waits for the golden-cheek. As these birds arrive, the flowers of the Texas redbuds are already fading and falling, as are those of the Mexican plum and the fragrant agarita. With marvelous timing, the golden-cheek's arrival coincides with the bursting of the buds of the Spanish oaks, a key element in their strict habitat requirements. With the first warm-up of early March, the oaks begin blossoming and issuing out the tiniest of leaves. Not surprisingly, this is the signal for a flush of insect activity. Innumerable butterfly larvae begin devouring those early oak leaves. Flies, bees, treehoppers, spiders, and a host of other choice morsels suddenly appear in abundance in, on, and around the developing foliage. The feast is on.

This rush to spring signals the start, for the warblers and their human admirers, of a frantically short season of activity. While the female warblers may arrive a week or so behind the males, they waste no time before settling into a chosen territory, beginning the business of building the nest from the thin strips of cedar bark, and preparing to raise their single brood of the year. Within a mere sixty to eighty days, the song of the male warblers, which started at such an up-tempo pace, will have declined to an occasional mumble.

By mid- to late May we begin to search with hopefulness for broods of noisy little fledglings taking their first hops through the cedar breaks. If a given pair fails in their first attempt, they often do not renest. If a female Brown-headed Cowbird has been successful in tricking the warblers into raising some of her own, the golden-cheek nestlings have a big strike against them; perhaps only a single warbler chick will be raised with its gluttonous cowbird sibling.

In yet another sixty days, by late July, we are hard-pressed to find golden-cheeks at all. Most of them have turned tail and headed south once again, leaving us to the heat of the late summer and showing us why we aptly call these birds "neotropical migrants." Is it presumptuous of us to claim the birds as native Texans when they spend only four to five months each year with us and the remainder of the year south of the border? Having expended so much biological effort to continue to breed, and to have adapted to accomplish this all in the shelter of our green-clad canyonlands in the Texas Hill Country, the Golden-cheeked Warbler is indeed deserving of special notice. I remain hopeful that the increased attention garnered in recent years by this bird has resulted in conservation efforts and a general raising of awareness that will serve as the foundation for the long-term survival of these gems of the Hill Country.

CHARLES SEXTON

© John P. O'Neill-1990

Yellow-breasted Chat and Japanese Honeysuckle

Icteria virens and *Lonicera japonica*

I HAVE NEVER BEEN COMPELLED to buy and replace optics because of a recurring fantasy. Someday, when I am too decrepit and deaf to bird, I will take my binoculars, which will probably be the ones I acquired from Edgar B. Kincaid in 1983, turn them upside down, shake them like a ketchup bottle, and all the birds I've seen through them will fall out on the table. One I will await with particular kinship will be the Yellow-breasted Chat.

I've always liked roundish birds with beady eyes. They have a certain boldness and ferocity that I admire and emulate. They remind me of my favorite obituary, for an ancient and venerable British book publisher named Sir Basil Blackwell, who shortly before his death ascribed his longevity to being "in a constant state of mild irritation." Every chat I've ever seen seems mildly irritated, as does every Northern Mockingbird, Yellow-eyed Junco, Black-capped Vireo, Green Jay, and Sedge Wren. I plead guilty to willful anthropomorphizing; these are my kinds of birds.

I think of the chat as one of my intimate compatriots. I carry one in my pocket. If I am lying insomniac in bed I can conjure up the yellow, for which my language has no suitable adjectives, and the song, which goes beyond melody. I have not seen many chats. It is a constant amazement to me that something so seldom seen can so amplify my life.

Early in my desultory birding career, the chat taught me a lesson about myself. I was happier letting birds come to me than I was pursuing them. While my beloved, immensely more talented, and, though I defend my own regard for birds as ardent enough, far more passionate friends crashed into the brush and saw the bird in question, I hung back. This meant I would forever reside on that lowest rung of birding, the one to which dilettantes cling.

Perhaps as a way of concealing a lack of talent, I developed a personal code. I would let a bird reveal itself to me when it was ready. Because of this doctrine, a bird, for me, is often a singing bush. And none is more so than the chat. It is an irascible little cantor in a thicket.

The most recent chat I did not see was along the Niobrara River in Nebraska in the summer of 1996. I was helping to lead a canoe trip of predominantly nonbirders on that lovely Great Plains river. We had stopped for a picnic at a state park shelter, and as I was accommodating and facilitating and doing what courteous trip leaders do, a chat began to flute and chortle and babble in the brush about ten feet from me and my tuna sandwich.

Like automatons, the only other bird watcher in the group and I dropped our conversations, jerked our heads, stood up, walked the few paces to the thicket, and started making squeaking and pishing noises to try to lure the chat out of its hiding place. This response, standard behavior among bird watchers, is a source of great amusement to people who do not share our avocation, and I am always mildly irritated that they find comical what I find so deeply fulfilling. The chat, continuing its ecstatic, arrhythmic song but failing to divulge even a glimpse of its black beady eye, was giving me great pleasure at the same time it was taunting me. How exactly do you pick up your sandwich and the threads of your conversation and explain to people a beautiful thing unseen?

SUZANNE WINCKLER

© John P. O'Neill · 1984

Hooded Warblers and Bald Cypress *Wilsonia citrina* and *Taxodium distichum*

MOST PEOPLE never even notice warblers, but for me they are the most endearing and attractive of all birds. Their colors are so bright. They are so vibrant and full of life. They have such distinct personalities. Roger Tory Peterson called them "the butterflies of the bird world." Like shorebirds, they perform prodigious annual migrations. Most of us see them only in passage and then, alas, all too briefly. At those times they brighten the most somber day and bring color, excitement, and pleasure to those who observe them.

Of all the warblers, the hooded is my special favorite. Growing up in Houston, I often birded the coastal migrant traps hoping to experience a "fallout," an event when thousands of birds would encounter inclement weather and take shelter. The Hooded Warblers would show up in late March and continue moving through until early May, but the peak numbers occurred in early April. On a good day we would see thirty or forty hoodeds.

Unlike such treetop warblers as the Blackburnian and the Black-throated Green, this species stays close to the ground. I have often seen hoodeds on the ground making short dashes in pursuit of flying insects. Seen at such close range, the pattern of the male is striking. The deep black hood frames an intensely yellow face that is so bright it seems to glow from within. The underparts are yellow; the back and tail, olive. The female lacks the black hood. White tail spots, typical of many warblers, are very pronounced in the hooded, especially since the tail is often flashed.

The Hooded Warbler breeds in mixed lowland forests that have a dense understory of shrubs. Its principal breeding ground is in the southeastern United States, but it has bred as far north as Minnesota and Connecticut. In Texas it breeds in the woodlands of East Texas. It occurs in small numbers as far west as Bastrop County and has bred as far south as Matagorda County. It winters mainly in the lowlands of southeast Mexico, Guatemala, Honduras, Nicaragua, and Costa Rica. Its preferred winter habitat is lowland rain forest, but it also occurs in adjacent areas of old second growth and on the grounds of motels that have sufficient trees. Male Hoodeds tend to winter further north than females.

As a teenager I spent many weekends at the Little Thicket Nature Sanctuary in San Jacinto County with my friend and mentor Joe Heiser. Joe had superb hearing and enjoyed bird song immensely. He taught me the song of the Hooded Warbler, which is regarded by many as one of the best songsters among the warblers. The great ornithologist Frank Chapman described its voice as *you must come to the woods or you won't see me.*

VICTOR EMANUEL

© John P. O'Neill - 1987

Painted Redstarts and Madrone *Myioborus pictus* and *Arbutus texana*

THE MORNING AIR had already climbed into the low nineties. A friend and I entered the cottonwood gallery surrounded by a chorus of songs from White-winged Dove, from Cactus, Canyon, and Bewick's Wrens, from Crissal Thrasher and cicadas. A flash of black and white high up in a cottonwood caught our eye, and our first impression was of a brightly colored butterfly attracted to fresh sap flow. Closer attention revealed one of the flashiest warblers in the New World. A Painted Redstart was hawking insects near the trunk, its moves very deliberate and showy. Outer white tail feathers fanned out and waved side to side as the bird moved. All of a sudden the red lower breast and upper belly blazed like a roaring fire against a mostly black body. If that wasn't enough, the large white wing patches flashed in unison with the tail movements as it uttered sharp call notes, reminiscent of a Pine Siskin's call.

So what was a Painted Redstart doing at this location in Big Bend Ranch State Park in early September? It was obviously a migrant, but where did it come from? The Painted Redstart is truly a borderlands bird, in summer occupying mountain islands of the southwestern deserts of Arizona, extreme southwestern New Mexico, and the Chisos Mountains of West Texas. In winter the species retreats south into Mexico. I have had the privilege of observing this bird at four locations in Texas and Mexico. In fact, I was present when the first known nesting record was documented for the Davis Mountains of Texas. The nest was a neat little straw-lined cup well hidden in a steep grassy bank in a pine-oak woodland. The Painted Redstart is a proud and deserving example of the rich diversity of the birds of Texas.

KELLY B. BRYAN

© John P. O'Neill · 1991

Altamira Oriole and Cedar Elm *Icterus gularis* and *Ulmus crassifolia*

THE BIRDER WHO is a newcomer to the wonderful opportunities afforded by the tropical woodlands of South Texas will soon encounter a delightful dilemma: trying to differentiate between the beautiful Altamira and Hooded Orioles. At first, the male hooded and both sexes of the Altamira seem maddeningly similar—orange about the head and underparts, with a black throat. The key is in the wing bars. Both wing bars are white in the Hooded Oriole. In the Altamira, the lower wing bar is white, and the upper is orange. But the birder who becomes familiar with the two species can tell them apart from a fair distance merely by shape. The Altamira is much stockier, and its bill is also stockier in proportion. The Altamira is more likely to perch in the open at the top of bare branches, usually exclaiming *ike, ike, ike,* a call very different from any of the hooded's.

In the early 1960s the Altamira (or Lichtenstein's Oriole, as it was then known) was not an easy bird to encounter in the South Texas woodlands. The Black-headed Oriole (also known as Audubon's Oriole) and the Hooded Oriole were much more readily seen. The hooded seemed to prefer more urban open areas, with palms the preferred nest tree. By the 1970s Audubon's and Hooded Orioles were in decline and the Altamira became fairly common, even moving into wooded residential areas, where its wonderful pendant sack nests hung suspended even from phone lines. Observers speculated that these nests and the bird's larger size enabled the Altamira Oriole to better withstand the great increase in Brown-headed and Red-eyed Cowbird populations during that time and the resulting nest parasitism, while the Hooded and Audubon's Orioles could not cope as well.

In the mid-1990s there are as many cowbirds as ever, but the Altamira has been in a slow decline over the last ten or fifteen years, while the hooded has made a small comeback in some urban areas during roughly the same time. The Altamira Oriole, preferring the deeper woodlands, is now probably suffering from human encroachment into the last remaining woodlands in South Texas.

It is wonderful, however, still to have some numbers of each of these strikingly beautiful orioles around, if only to keep those birding skills sharp.

F. P. "TONY" BENNETT

Summer Tanager and Bromeliad *Piranga rubra* and *bromeliad*

YOU MIGHT THINK it surprising that the first thing a person notices about a bright-red bird is something other than its color. But this is what happened the first time Karen encountered a Summer Tanager. It was in the Big Thicket area of Hardin County, a few years before we met. Karen had been censusing the birds there all winter and now it was spring. On a bright April morning, from high in a white oak, came a clear, flutelike song. What could it be? A robin? A thrush? Such a lovely, distinctive song, which Karen committed to memory as she scanned the canopy. Why, there it was! A completely red bird, but not a cardinal. This was a new arrival—a migrant just back from wintering in the tropics. The cardinals had been singing since February, but they never sounded like this. This song was rich and liquid, flowing out over the treetops. Seeing the bird's yellowish bill, its sturdy body, its redness unlike the red of a cardinal, Karen knew it then for what it was: a tanager, a tropical bird coming to nest in the food-rich temperate forests during the warm summer. This songster was a summer redbird, the Summer Tanager.

As dramatic as the song of the Summer Tanager is, its call may be even more distinctive. Each spring we hear *chick-i-tuck, chicky-took* emanating from the tall trees around our small farm, and we know that our pair of Summer Tanagers has returned. As they deliberately forage for beetles and flying insects, they call to each other repeatedly. Summer Tanagers breed in a broad swath across the middle of Texas, from the forests and thickets of East Texas westward to the Trans-Pecos, where they prefer the cottonwoods of stream bottoms. A few individuals can be found in South Texas, but it is not really a brush-country species. In these areas the Summer Tanager chooses patches of live oak in which to forage and nest.

The Summer Tanager winters from southern Mexico to Amazonia and is noted for its eclectic choice of habitat in the tropics. Although it rarely sings on the winter range, its characteristic call can be heard from mangrove thickets to coffee plantations and from sea level to elevations of more than six thousand feet in the humid mountains.

As we compose these words, a late-November blue norther is blowing into Texas. How we anticipate those warmer April days when the chick-i-tucks, as we like to call them, return to our backyard!

ROBERT AND KAREN BENSON

Northern Cardinals, Goldenrod, and Mistflower

Cardinalis cardinalis, Solidago sp., and *Eupatorium coelestinum*

MOST FOLKS KNOW IT as the redbird. Officially, it is the Northern Cardinal. The Northern Cardinal ranges throughout the eastern half of the United States to about the 100th meridian, along the lower reaches of the southwestern border states to the Pacific, and through much of Mexico to northern Guatemala and Belize. So where is a "southern" cardinal?

The only other North American bird in the genus *Cardinalis* is the Pyrrhuloxia (*Cardinalis sinuatus*), which occupies more arid terrain throughout the Northern Cardinal's range in the Southwest and in northern Mexico. One must look beyond Panama to find the Vermilion Cardinal (*Cardinalis phoeniceus*) of northern South America, which, with our *Cardinalis cardinalis*—it is postulated—constitutes a superspecies. The Vermilion Cardinal is the only member of the genus *Cardinalis* in South America.

The word "cardinal" evokes the image of a cleric of the Roman Catholic Church, robed in red. Actually, the word "cardinal" derives from the Greek *cardo,* translated "hinge"—or "something of prime importance." *Cardinalis phoeniceus* seems more aptly named. *Phoeniceus* derives from the Greek *phoinix,* "crimson," alluding to the Phoenicians, who first discovered and used the color.

The male cardinal, with its red robe, black face, and prominent crest, is one of the most readily noticed and identified of all our native bird species. The female, a modest buffy-brown color, is tinged with red only on her wings, tail, and crest.

The male is a fine songster, which is contrary to the behavior of numerous species, in which the males seem to use vocal skills to compensate for drab appearance. Song phrases are highly variable, but the pattern and the loud, clear, whistled notes render the presentation easily identifiable. Unlike many sexually dimorphic species, the female sings as well as the male; however, the singing often goes unnoticed—in part because it is largely confined to the courtship period.

It is during courtship that the cardinal shows behavior that endears it to the human observer. If you have a feeder frequented by cardinals during the winter, you will have noticed that the male ignores the female. But once courtship is under way the pair will share the feeder—the male frequently sidling over to the female and gently placing a sunflower seed in her beak. This solicitous behavior continues at the nest, where the male may bring food to both his mate and the young. And when the fledglings of the first brood have left the nest, the male tends the troupe with great diligence while the female is concerned with a second nesting.

The Northern Cardinal is doing quite well at a time when many bird populations are declining. The species is nonmigratory and so is not subject to the many hazards endured by migratory songbirds. Nor is it greatly affected by forest loss and fragmentation.

Several states—Illinois, Indiana, Kentucky, North Carolina, Virginia, and West Virginia—have claimed the Northern Cardinal as their state bird. Surely it is appreciated wherever it enthralls the observer with its beauty and song.

FRED WEBSTER

Pyrrhuloxias and Mesquite   *Cardinalis sinuatus* and *Prosopis glandulosa*

DECEMBER 1974. We've spent the day driving from Austin to the Rio Grande Valley. In the way of all car-bound bird watchers, we jerk toward our destination, stopping and starting like clowns in a circus car, doors popping open, binoculars and scopes pouring out. A friend would later draw a cartoon of this typical scene; in frame after frustrating frame, birders hop in and out of a little round car on an endless progression toward a lunch that never materializes. We break all the Bird Watchers' Rules: "Never bird in the rain." "Never stop for a passerine on a wire." "Never turn around for a small brown bird." Never mind—the chase is the thing. The possibilities are as endless as the drive. The company is good. Today, the warm-up day before our official Christmas Bird Count, is for us. Pyrrhuloxias forage in the thornbush as we drive into Falcon State Recreation Area; their flocks steal from mesquite to mesquite and flutter in the acacias as we set up for the night.

The Pyrrhuloxia encapsulates the less-than-spectacular but nonetheless intense beauty of Texas' Rio Grande Valley. Hard to appreciate if you are looking for drama, the Pyrrhuloxia's quiet colors are those of the desert at dawn, of the one neon sign glowing along Rio Grande City's empty main street. Like the Valley itself, the Pyrrhuloxia reveals little at first glance that would command a second glance. But only those who take the time for a second glance discover this bird's appeal. The Valley is a similarly magical blend of romance and reality. Far from being in-your-face gorgeous, its dusty scrubbiness upholds the trailer courts among citrus orchards, the *vato*-filled dance halls along farm-to-market roads, and the *madre*-and-*padre* taco stands as icons of gritty beauty.

We are a bit dusty and scrubby ourselves, and though we don't know it yet, our night's sleep will be ruined by bass fishers competing in a louder and different Christmas Count. We have varied interests and eccentricities, buried dramas and intentions. But we are already happily submerged in Trip Mode, that chat-and-chew ritual of jokes and road food and hyperbole with which every group of friends celebrates a journey, and no one's feelings are hurt when the sight of another bird in the clearing interrupts the current story—this being the test that divides real birders from recreational ones. The birders' passionate litany of species seen and species suspected rises and falls along with news of human friends and events, and the Pyrrhuloxias nibble seeds along the pavement by the side of our shelter as we pull cheese and bread and beer from the ice chest. They are as tough and enduring as the Valley. More than twenty years later, we are too.

HOLLY CARVER

© John P. O'Neill · 1984

Painted Buntings and Macartney Rose *Passerina ciris* and *Rosa bracteata*

FRED GRASPED MY HAND and raced me across the University of Texas campus to the northeast corner of Twenty-first and Guadalupe Streets. There, an open area of short grass and scattered trees had been neglected by grounds-keepers, and the air seemed alive with small birds flitting between trees and grass, where they fed on matured seed. Some birds were bright blue, some greenish, some brownish—but most striking were those with blue head, red under-parts and rump, and yellowish-green back. We were spellbound. What were these birds? Where were they from? Why were they here on this overcast April day?

Fortunately, we knew to contact W. D. "Bill" Anderson, who readily identified our birds over the phone: Painted Buntings, Indigo Buntings, Clay-colored Sparrows. Overnight thunder-storms had forced these migrants down, and they had converged on the nearest area where they could feed and rest.

Bill and Agatha Anderson would become our mentors, leading us into a lifelong interest in birds. Through them we were introduced to Connie Hagar and Rockport birding, a high point in our early learning period.

Our reaction to the Painted Bunting has been shared by many people seeing this small bird for the first time. Early ornithologists described the bunting as being shy, but those of us who live in areas where it commonly nests and migrates find it to be quite active and visible—certainly not shy. I have mental images of the male singing his melodious warble from exposed perches, on tall grass stalks in open woodland, from the highest tree in streamside forest, his colors high-lighted by the morning sun.

Persons who claim never to have seen the male may not be very observant, as birds come readily to garden feeders and baths. On the other hand, one may be excused for not noticing the female, whose bright olive-green and greenish yellow plumage blends well with the thick greenery in which she places her nest.

The Painted Bunting breeds throughout Louisiana, Arkansas, southwestern Missouri, and most of Oklahoma and Texas, and in northern Mexico from Chihuahua to Tamaulipas, avoiding more arid regions. A population is also found on a coastal strip from southeastern North Carolina to central florida. A relatively few remain to winter in the United States.

The male is very pugnacious in defense of his breeding territory, and battles between males are often bloody—sometimes fatal. This behavior makes them easy to trap, and in the 1800s and early 1900s it was the most frequently caged bird in the South.

The Painted Bunting's preferred food is the seeds of grass and weeds, which constitute 80 percent of its diet. The remaining 20 percent is composed of insects, including the boll weevil. These food choices, along with its preferred habitat, indicate that the Painted Bunting could be adversely affected by recent agricultural practices in Texas, especially the clearing of fencerows and the use of chemicals. Our department of agriculture mounted a massive spraying of malathion on cotton fields in 1995, which turned out to be the most disastrous season for cotton farmers in sixty years.

Destruction and fragmentation of bunting habitat are particularly noticeable in Central Texas as the human population explodes. Along with this general trend, the University of Texas has built on our "bunting corner," and little open space remains for overnight drop-ins.

MARIE WEBSTER

Black-throated Sparrow and Tasajillo *Amphispiza bilineata* and *Opuntia leptocaulis*

ON MY FIRST TRIP through West Texas many years ago, I approached the Pecos River crossing and decided to take a break from my long day of driving. I turned off on a side road to the river's overlook to enjoy one of the state's most impressive scenic views. As soon as I got out of my car, I began hearing this distinctive bird song. I never forgot the sound: two clear opening notes, followed by a fine trill, *cheet cheet cheeeeeeee.* I walked toward the sound along the slopes of the river, where the terrain was rocky with scattered cactus, ocotillo, yucca, and creosote bush. Suddenly I was greeted once again with the song, and perched right in front of me, on top of a prickly pear cactus, was a very handsome sparrow. The bird was dark gray above and light gray below, with white facial stripes and a jet-black throat. This was my first look at the Black-throated Sparrow, the most beautiful sparrow I had ever seen. I was especially taken by the contrasting black and white markings that make this bird such an eye-catcher.

Once appropriately called the desert sparrow, this bird occurs in deserts, particularly along rocky slopes, throughout the southwestern United States from Wyoming and California south to Mexico and eastward to Central Texas. In Texas, the Black-throated Sparrow breeds from March through September, and many pairs may raise two broods a year. The nest consists of a loose cup of grasses, typically in cactus or low brush, in which the female will lay three to four whitish eggs. Its food includes various seeds, small grasshoppers, and other insects.

As I reluctantly left the Pecos River overlook, the song of the Black-throated Sparrow played over and over in my head. Still today, when I am fortunate enough to be passing through this part of Texas, I make it a point to stop at the overlook to pay a visit to an old handsome friend of the desert and enjoy listening to its song.

RANDELL BEAVERS

The Artist

John P. O'Neill was born in Houston in 1942. In 1948 his parents purchased two acres in the "country" west of Houston. Soon afterward, a friend gave him bantam chickens, and a few years later he received a trio of Golden Pheasants. These events, plus the proximity of fields and woods, probably steered him into a love and fascination for birds. At the age of five he finished his first painting, a bantam chicken that he copied from a card and gave to his mother.

O'Neill's choice of the University of Oklahoma for undergraduate studies was mainly influenced by the presence there of George M. Sutton—ornithologist, naturalist, and renowned painter of birds. In 1961, while on a Fulbright, O'Neill spent the summer with friends in Peru, an expedition that permanently set his life's course. On this first trip, he made a small collection of birds from the Amazonian part of the country. Upon his return to the United States, Sutton suggested the collection be deposited at the Louisiana State University Museum of Natural Science, where George H. Lowery Jr. and his students were becoming involved in studies of tropical birds.

O'Neill has continued his research in Peru ever since. In more than thirty-five years of expeditions and explorations, O'Neill has described thirteen species of birds new to science, more than any living person. After completing his undergraduate studies at University of Oklahoma, he went on to get his M.S. and Ph.D. at Louisiana State.

In 1974 he was appointed a curator for the bird and mammal collections at the L.S.U. Museum of Natural Science, and in 1978 he was appointed its director. However, administrative work was not O'Neill's choice of professional pursuits. He soon took a part-time position at L.S.U. and began to spend more time painting. He now supports himself mainly through the sale of his work, which has been published in hundreds of magazines, books, articles, newspapers, and other publications and has been exhibited in museums throughout the United States, as well as in many foreign countries. In the future, O'Neill hopes to be able to continue his fieldwork and research in Peru, as well as to paint as long as he is able to do so.

The Contributors

Leticia A. Alamía grew up in the Lower Rio Grande Valley. An early affinity for animals of all kinds decreed a biological career. It was Dr. Pauline James's zoology class at Pan American College (now UT–Pan American) that steered Letty Alamía toward field biology and animal behavior. Dr. James also provided contact with many ornithologists, conservation leaders, bird watchers, and other students (including Alamía's future husband, John O'Neill). Alamía spent several years with the American Peace Corps Environmental Program in Iran and has worked with state and federal wildlife agencies, zoos, and nature centers. She writes on the subject of pet behavior management and counsels owners about problem pet behavior. She also assists her husband in birding tours and field expeditions to South America.

Keith Arnold is professor of wildlife and fisheries sciences at Texas A&M University and curator of birds for the Texas Cooperative Wildlife Collections. Arnold received his Ph.D. at Louisiana State University under the direction of the late George Lowery Jr., graduating in 1996. He began his career that same year at Texas A&M. His research interests include the systematics, ecology, and distributions of Texas birds, bird-human interactions, and neotropical ornithology. His research has included work in Costa Rica, the Dominican Republic, and the Commonwealth of Dominica.

John Arvin began a lifelong obsession with birds as a young child. When his family moved to the lower Rio Grande Valley in the late 1950s, he was first exposed to the electrifying excitement of the birds of the neotropics. He has pursued several occupations related to the environment, most notably fifteen years as a full-time leader of birding tours. He has served on the Texas Ornithological Society's Bird Records Committee since its inception and currently holds the position of chair. Most recently, Arvin has worked as seasonal resident naturalist in Amazonian Peru, and he continues to write about and photograph birds and other natural history subjects of that region.

Randell Beavers is currently the director of the Spring Branch ISD Science Center in Houston, Texas. He grew up in Houston and has been birding in Texas for twenty-eight years. Randy Beavers' love for West Texas is evidenced by the numerous Science Center birding tours he has led to the region since 1978.

Roy Bedichek (1878–1959) was born in Illinois but moved with his family to Falls County, Texas, in 1884 and attended school at his father's academy in Eddy. For thirty years, Bedichek worked with the University Interscholastic League. While visiting schools throughout Texas during that time, he got into the habit of camping and became enamored of the outdoors and of wildlife, particularly birds. In 1947 he wrote *Adventures with a Texas Naturalist,* a classic work of nature writing and conservationist sensibility, which is still in print (University of Texas Press).

Robert Behrstock has been based in Houston since 1980. Formerly a fisheries biologist in Northern California, he has led birding tours for the last nineteen years, primarily in Latin America. Bob Behrstock is keenly interested in photographing and tape-recording birds, especially nightbirds. Most recently, he has turned his photographic and writing skills toward dragonflies.

F. P. "Tony" Bennett grew up in the small West Texas town of Marfa, where he learned about birds while sighting along the barrel of a BB gun. Later, at age ten, a move to Harlingen in South Texas led to the gun's being replaced by binoculars and an avid, lifelong interest in just watching and painting. He has been painting birds since childhood. After traveling to tropical Mexico in his teenage years, Bennett has specialized in the birds of the neotropics. In his thirty years as a professional artist, he has provided illustrations for many books and articles on birds, and his original and printed work is in numerous private and corporate collections.

Robert and Karen Benson have lived most of their lives in Texas. Both of them began noticing birds and wildlife at an early age. Robert vividly remembers finding a copy of Peterson's *A Field Guide to the Birds of North America* in the school library and, on his way home that day, identifying his first bird—an American Robin. He went on to earn his Ph.D. in cosmic ray physics at Texas A&M University in 1985. During that time he kept his feet on the ground by bird watching and banding. Later he coupled his love of physics with his love of birds by founding the Center for Bioacoustics. The center (now housed at Texas A&M University at Corpus Christi) investigates and archives all sorts of natural sounds, including bird songs. Karen earned her degree in biology while studying fruit flies at the University of Texas. She finally came around to birds while exploring the Big Thicket during her graduate studies at Lamar University. Robert and Karen met in 1985 while bird watching in the Sabine Woods Bird Sanctuary, and they've been together ever since.

Jim Bones is a landscape photographer, writer, and teacher whose work deals primarily with natural history and sustainable environments. He has published many magazine portfolios, articles, and books relating to North American wildlands, including *Texas Heartland: A Hill Country Year, Texas West of the Pecos, Rio Grande: Mountains to the Sea, Wildflowers across America,* and *Seeds of Change: The Living Treasure.* Bones's fine-art dye transfer prints are in many private and public collections, including those at the Amon Carter Museum, the University of Texas, Rice University, and Southwest Texas State University. He currently lives in Marathon, Texas.

David Braun is a native Texan and lifelong naturalist. He currently lives in Austin, where he is working as a management consultant and developing environmental business ventures. From 1988 until 1995, he served as the director of The Nature Conservancy of Texas. During 1987 and 1988, he helped open the office of the Environmental Defense Fund in Texas. Braun was an attorney for the Texas Parks and Wildlife Department and, before that, a nature tour leader with Victor Emanuel Nature Tours and Field Guides. He has a B.A. in biochemistry from the University of Texas at Austin and a law degree from the University of Texas School of Law.

Michael Braun is a curator of birds and director of the Laboratory of Molecular Systematics at the National Museum of Natural History, Smithsonian Institution. His scientific research concerns the evolutionary history and relationships of birds, especially in the neotropics. He grew up in Houston and began watching birds in high school with his brother, David, and friends Orlyn Gaddis, Dan Hardy, and Victor Emanuel. He now lives in Maryland with his wife, Kirsten, and daughters, Jessica and Julia.

Kelly B. Bryan was hooked the very first time he went on a bird walk, when he was twelve years old. As a teenager he taught himself to identify birds in and around the Central Texas town of Mart, where he lived in the 1960s. College was interrupted by service as a communications and Vietnamese-language specialist in the U.S. Army until 1973. Bryan finished a master's degree in 1979 at Sam Houston State University. His recordings of bird songs provided the impetus for the establishment of the Texas Bird Sound Library, housed at Sam Houston State University. Since 1976 Bryan has worked for the Texas Parks and Wildlife Department, most recently as regional resource coordinator for Trans-Pecos Texas state parks.

Holly Carver, a native Texan, was introduced to bird watching when she helped proofread *The Bird Life of Texas* in the early 1970s. Formerly a manuscript editor at the University of Texas Press, she is now director at the University of Iowa Press in Iowa City.

Fred Collins is director of the Hana and Arthur Ginzbarg Nature Discovery Center in Bellaire, Texas. A native Houstonian, he is a graduate of the Texas A&M Wildlife and Fisheries Sciences Department. Collins does consulting work, most often with endangered species of birds, including Piping Plover, Mountain Plover, and Eskimo Curlew. He and his wife, Kassie, maintain a flock of more than thirty species of parrots at his Center for Avian Propagation and Research. He is a past president of the Houston Audubon Society.

Robin Doughty became fascinated by birds when he was growing up on the North Sea coast of Holderness, England. There, "sea watches" and observations of bird passage through a local mere impressed upon him the mobility of waterbird species and led him to study bird migration in Mediterranean Europe, Africa, Australia, and Latin America. Currently, Robin is a professor in the Department of Geography at the University of Texas at Austin, and he has authored books on famous North American birds, including the Whooping Crane and the Northern Mockingbird, both published by the University of Texas Press.

Victor Emanuel started birding in Texas at the age of eight. His travels have taken him to all the continents, with his areas of concentration being Texas, Arizona, Mexico, Panama, and Peru. He is the founder and compiler for forty years of the Freeport Christmas Bird Count and has served a term as president of the Texas Ornithological Society. He holds a B.A. in zoology and botany from the University of Texas and an M.A. in government from Harvard. Emanuel initiated the first birding camps for young people, and he considers that one of his greatest achievements. He is a leader of bird tours and lives in Austin.

Ted Lee Eubanks, who lives in Austin, is president of Texas Partners in Flight, a member of the board of directors of the National Audubon Society, and an advisory board member of the National Fish and Wildlife Foundation. Eubanks has formerly served as president of the Houston Audubon Society, the Texas Ornithological Society, and Armand Bayou Nature Center. He is involved in studying and promoting nature tourism as a sustainable economic approach for communities.

Ben Feltner began birding as a child in England. He lived and birded in Texas from 1950 to 1984, during which time he monitored spring and fall migration annually on the Texas coast. He fondly remembers being the only birder present at High Island during an April "fallout." The high point of his sojourn in Texas occurred on March 22, 1959, when he and his friend D. A. Deaver rediscovered the Eskimo Curlew on Galveston Island. He spent more than twenty years leading birding tours, most of them in Texas. Feltner currently lives in Seattle with his artist wife, Linda, and their two Dobermans.

Ernest Franzgrote lives in Vermont. Together with artist F. P. "Tony" Bennett of Harlingen, Texas, he is writing a book on all the hummingbirds. He has traveled widely in Central and South America and for the past seven years has studied the behavior of hummers using a video camera. Franzgrote grew up in Illinois and then worked for many years at a NASA center in California. He helped develop the instrument that, thirty years ago, gave the first elemental analysis of the moon's surface. This experiment, in rejuvenated form, arrived on Mars in 1997 aboard the rover

Sojourner. In his final years before retirement he served as science team chief of the *Voyager* project. Like the Ruby-throated Hummingbird, he has flown under his own power (but only about eight hundred feet in a pedal-powered aircraft).

Fred Gehlbach is professor emeritus of biology and environmental studies at Baylor University, where he taught for thirty-two years. His bird studies in Texas span the last forty-five years. His population work on suburban Eastern Screech Owls in Waco is now in its thirty-second year.

Bill Graber is a retired urologic surgeon who lives in Beaumont. He has served as vice president of the American Birders Association and as publisher of the organization's *Birding Magazine.* He is a past president of the Texas Ornithological Society and former chairman of the board of trustees of The Nature Conservancy of Texas.

John Graves was born in Texas a long time ago. He believed during a couple of stages of his life that he had perhaps escaped from that background, but—quite happily in the long run—this turned out not to be so. With his wife, Jane, he continues to live on a hilly, rock-strewn stock farm in north central Texas, watches birds about as ignorantly as ever, goes fishing, and still does some writing on occasion.

Stephen Harrigan is a novelist, journalist, and screenwriter. A former senior editor for *Texas Monthly,* he is the author of five books, including *A Natural State, Comanche Midnight,* and *Water and Light: A Diver's Journey to a Coral Reef* (University of Texas Press). He lives in Austin, where he is currently at work on a novel about the Alamo.

Sally Graves Jackson, born and raised in Texas, studied biology and English at Rice University and attended graduate school in wildlife ecology at Utah State University. She has done field research on songbirds and waterfowl in Yellowstone National Park, California, and Utah. She has also taught outdoor science programs for several organizations, including the National Audubon Society and the California Marine Mammal Center. She is now a contributing writer at *Utah State University Magazine* and lives in Durham, North Carolina, with her husband and two young boys.

Dr. Pauline James, known as "Doc" to most of her students, came to South Texas shortly after completing her Ph.D. at Cornell University in Ithaca, New York. She joined the Department of Biology at Pan American University in Edinburg (now the University of Texas–Pan American) in 1953 and lived in the Valley until her death in 1995. She was a naturalist, a bird watcher, and a diligent and outspoken conservationist, and she inspired many to follow in her footsteps. Among her conservation accomplishments, she helped protect the Anzalduas natural area and was a founder of the Frontera Audubon Society and the Valley Nature Center.

Kenn Kaufman, a lifelong bird watcher, lives in Tucson, Arizona, but has made annual birding trips to Texas since the early 1970s. A freelance writer, illustrator, and speaker on bird subjects, he has written scores of magazine articles as well as four books, including *Kingbird Highway* and *Lives of North American Birds.*

Edgar B. Kincaid Jr. (1921–1985) was born in San Antonio and grew up on a ranch in the Hill Country, where he was attracted to the natural world rather than to the world of cattle and horses. The *Burgess Bird Book for Children,* purchased for him by his mother when he was about six, was the beginning of a lifelong obsession with birds and books about birds. His extensive ornithological library now resides at Texas A&M University. Kincaid edited Harry Church Oberholser's *The Bird Life of Texas,* published in 1974 by the University of Texas Press.

Edward A. Kutac is a retired accountant who now lives in Amarillo. His birding avocation began in 1963 and continues. He is a past president of the Travis Audubon Society and the Texas Ornithological Society. Kutac is the author of *Birder's Guide to Texas* and the coauthor of *Birds and Other Wildlife of South Central Texas.* He taught a bird-identification class in Austin for about seventeen years and now teaches a similar class in Amarillo.

Stephen E. "Chip" Labuda Jr. grew up in Kingsville and began bird watching at seven years of age. He was educated in parochial and public schools in Kingsville and Corpus Christi. He has earned two college degrees: a B.S. in biology from Texas A&I University in 1971 and an M.S. in wildlife and fisheries science from Texas A&M University in 1977. He has spent twenty-four years in federal service, twenty of those with the U.S. Fish and Wildlife Service, working on refuges. All of Labuda's refuge experience has been in Texas and includes work on Aransas, Santa Ana, Attwater Prairie Chicken, and Laguna Atascosa National Wildlife Refuges. He still enjoys bird watching and uses it as an excuse to make monthly trips into Mexico. When he travels on official assignments to such destinations as Albuquerque, New Mexico, Washington, D.C., and Minneapolis, Minnesota, he always packs a pair of binoculars.

Greg Lasley first formed an interest in birds as a Boy Scout in the early 1960s. After moving to Texas in the early 1970s, he became seriously involved in Texas birding and in 1983 he became the coeditor, with Chuck Sexton, for the Texas region for *American Birds* (now *ABA Field Notes*), a publication of the American Birding Association. In this position, as well as that of the secretary of the Texas Bird Records Committee of the Texas Ornithological Society, Lasley has gained a deep love and knowledge of the birds of Texas. After a twenty-five-year career as a law enforcement officer he retired and is now a tour leader for Victor Emanuel Nature Tours.

Terry C. Maxwell lives in San Angelo, Texas, where he was born. He is a professor of biology at Angelo State University, teaching various courses in vertebrate zoology. He began watching birds at the age of twelve and has studied birds professionally since the age of nineteen, when he wrote his first scientific note.

June Osborne is a naturalist and freelance writer who lives in Waco. She has been watching and studying the birds of Texas since 1975, and writing about birds since 1980. Although she has traveled throughout Latin America and has led birding tours in Central America, her "special place" is on the Edwards Plateau in the Texas Hill Country, where she escapes whenever possible and where she conducts birding Elderhostels in the spring. Osborne is the author of three books: *Birder's Guide to Concan, Texas (and Surrounding Area), The Cardinal,* and *The Ruby-Throated Hummingbird.*

Jim Peterson is currently the director of technology at the Episcopal School of Dallas and adjunct curator of ornithology at the Dallas Museum of Natural History. He has worked for the National Audubon Society in Connecticut and has been involved in environmental education for the last fifteen years. His interest in neotropical birds has taken him to several Central and South American countries. He lives in Dallas with his wife, Gretchen, and has coauthored the book *Birds of the Trans-Pecos.*

Father Tom Pincelli is a Catholic priest with the Diocese of Brownsville. He has been actively birding since 1972, after he was "introduced" to the sport by a close friend and parishioner. He currently writes a weekly birding column for the three major Rio Grande Valley newspapers and is an executive board member for the Rio Grande Valley Birding Festival, held each year in Harlingen.

Rochelle Plasse was introduced to birds at an early age while helping tend her grandfather's flock of racing pigeons in Holbrook, Long Island. Pigeons led to dogs and cats, a ten-year after-school job as a veterinary technician, ownership of a full-line pet shop in New York City, and eighteen years as a staff member at the Houston Zoological Gardens. As curator of birds (a position she held for seven years), Plasse helped to develop field and captive husbandry protocols for various species, from Hawaiian honeycreepers to, most recently, Attwater's Prairie Chickens. She is also internationally known for her conservation work with curassows, guans, and chachalacas. In 1997 she became zoological manager of birds at Disney's Animal Kingdom in Orlando, Florida.

John Rowlett is a native of Austin and was one of the three editors of H. C. Oberholser's *The Bird Life of Texas* (1974), on which he worked closely with senior editor Edgar B. Kincaid Jr. and Suzanne Winckler. He has taught at the University of Virginia, where he received a doctorate in English. In 1985 Rowlett participated in forming Field Guides, an Austin-based birding-tour company for which he guides worldwide and serves as a director. He and his wife, Abbie, live in Charlottesville, Virginia; his daughter, Monica, lives in Austin.

Rose Ann Rowlett has an enduring interest in birds. From childhood days in Austin, birding by bicycle with her brother, John, until today, as she guides birding tours worldwide (still including Texas!), she has had the extreme good fortune of sharing her passion with others. Now living in San Diego, she works with Field Guides, an Austin-based birding-tour company that she helped found in 1985.

Peter Scott grew up in Durham, North Carolina, and graduated from Yale University with a degree in English. After working as a naturalist at Zion and Big Bend National Parks, he studied biology at the University of Texas (M.A.) and Louisiana State University (Ph.D.). His research includes the breeding biology of Turquoise-browed Motmots, the pollination ecology of hummingbird plants, the effects of prescribed fire in desert grassland, and the suitability of reclaimed strip mines for grassland birds. He and his wife, fellow biologist Diana Hews, teach and do research in the Department of Life Sciences at Indiana State University in Terre Haute.

Charles Sexton developed his childhood interest in the natural world on the beaches, bays, and rolling hills of Southern California. The overcrowding, taming, and disappearance of so much of that terrain led to his educational focus on human impacts on ecological systems. He transplanted to Austin in 1974, where he immersed himself in a new set of habitats facing similar threats. He completed a doctoral degree from the University of Texas at Austin in 1987. Chuck Sexton writes and edits the Texas regional columns for *ABA Field Notes* (and previously *American Birds*) with friend and colleague Greg Lasley. Currently, he is a wildlife biologist for the U.S. Fish and Wildlife Service at the Balcones Canyonlands National Wildlife Refuge.

Douglas Slack received a B.S. from Bowling Green State University and M.S. and Ph.D. degrees from Ohio State University. He has been at Texas A&M University since 1973 and is a professor in the Department of Wildlife and Fisheries Sciences. His research has focused on wetlands and wetlands-related migratory birds. He has published on Texas coastal birds, including colonial waterbirds, geese, and the endangered Whooping Crane. He is a member of numerous professional societies, including the American Ornithologists' Union, the Ecological Society of America, the Society for Conservation Biology, and the Wildlife Society.

James A. Tucker is an educator by profession. He is currently a professor of educational psychology at Andrews University, Berrien Springs, Michigan. Formerly he was president of Educational Directions, Incorporated, in Austin, and before that he held the position of program administrator with the Texas Education Agency. His avocation is natural history, particularly birds. He is the founder of the American Birding Association, serving as its executive director for eighteen years, and the founder of *Birding Magazine,* serving as its editor for sixteen years. Tucker has served as an officer or member of the board of four different Audubon societies in Florida and Texas.

Paul Turner showed up on a variety of jobs over several decades but was either too crazy or dim-witted to be much good at any of them. Resenting authority and unable to sit still for more than thirty minutes at a stretch, he barely survived the rigors associated with undergraduate education and broke down completely at the graduate level. He is now a naturalist, which is all he ever wanted to be anyway. He's self-employed, with a listing in the business pages of the Austin phone book. When not under hire, he does botany for fun and in this capacity has produced *The Flora of Walnut Creek Park.* He lives in Sunset Valley, Texas, with his wife, Molly; dogs, Piggy and Lulu; and cats, Data and Kitty Dooley.

John and Gloria Tveten live in Baytown, Texas, and have been ardent birders for more than thirty-five years. A former research chemist, John left that profession in 1973 to work as a full-time freelance nature writer and photographer and tour leader for the Smithsonian Institution and other organizations. Gloria retired from teaching college math to share more fully in these pursuits. Together, they write a weekly column, "Nature Trails," that has appeared in the *Houston Chronicle* since 1975. They are also the authors of several books on Texas birds, butterflies, and wildflowers.

Roland "Ro" Wauer is a nature writer living in Victoria, to which he moved after retiring from the National Park Service after a thirty-two-year career. He worked as a park naturalist in six national park units, including Crater Lake, Pinnacles, Death Valley, Zion, and Big Bend; in natural resource management in the Great Smoky Mountains and the Virgin Islands; as regional chief scientist in the Southwest Region Office in Santa Fe; and as chief of natural resources in Washington, D.C. Having visited every national park in the United States and Canada, Wauer claims that his all-time favorite park is Big Bend in West Texas. He has authored twelve books on birds and nature since his retirement.

Fred Webster endured an undistinguished career until he discovered birds in the spring of 1952. Intensive fieldwork in the Austin area quickly led to bestowal of the title "local expert," and while still damp behind the auriculars, he was urged into the position of South Texas regional editor for *ABA Field Notes* (then *American Birds*)—a prestigious honor for a struggling novice. The novelty soon wore off, but the ensuing struggle dragged on for twenty-five years. Another twenty-five years (with some overlap) followed of teaching noncredit bird-watching classes for various agencies. Mexican avifauna came to the fore in 1964 on Webster's first visit—with wife, Marie—to the cloud forest of southwestern Tamaulipas, Mexico. Bird study at Rancho del Cielo soon led to conducting nature tours to the region— now included in the El Cielo Biosphere Reserve—to benefit the biological research station.

Marie Webster has been curious about flowers, birds, and other creatures since childhood. As an adult, she found a focal point for her life in the wonders of nature. Early on, she benefited greatly from friendships with such legendary birders as Edgar Kincaid Jr., Connie Hagar, and L. Irby Davis. Over the years she has guided many visiting birders around Central Texas and assisted her husband, Fred, on class field trips. Her study of the breeding birds at Rancho del Cielo, in Mexico's northernmost tropical cloud forest, was published in *American Birds* (now *ABA Field Notes*). She and her husband have led nature tours to this region of Mexico since 1970. At home, she raises orchids and leads tours at the Lady Bird Johnson Wildflower Center in Austin.

Suzanne Winckler is a native Texan who began watching birds in the 1970s while working with Edgar B. Kincaid Jr. and John Rowlett on editing *The Bird Life of Texas*. She and her husband, David Smith, currently live in Omaha, Nebraska, where she works for The Nature Conservancy and does freelance writing, mainly about nature.

David E. Wolf is a longtime Texas birder who grew up in San Antonio and now lives in the Piney Woods of East Texas. After learning about the birds of the United States and Mexico for fifteen years, he was led by an interest in the mammals of Africa to East Africa in 1975, where he spent more than a year studying the birds and wildlife. In 1977 he began leading birding tours, specializing in the American West, Central America, Ecuador, and Africa. Wolf compiles several Christmas Bird Counts and regularly contributes field notes, but he especially enjoys his daily birding walks around the small farm in Nacogdoches that he shares with his wife, Mimi, their two children, and assorted horses, dogs, and cats.

Lawrence Wright, a staff writer for *The New Yorker,* is the author of five books, most recently *Twins: And What They Tell Us About Who We Are* (Wiley). Raised in Oklahoma and Texas, Wright lives now in Austin with his wife and children. He was introduced to the love of birds by his father, and he counts himself lucky to have many naturalists among his friends who can tell him what he's looking at.